T0207566

Thomas Piketty's
Capital in the Twenty-First Century

Thomas Piketty's
Capital in the Twenty-First Century

An Introduction

STEPHAN KAUFMANN
AND INGO STÜTZLE

Translated by Alexander Locascio

VERSO
London • New York

The translation of this work was supported by a
grant from the Goethe-Institut London.

This English-language edition first published by Verso 2017
Originally published in German as *Kapitalismus:*
Die ersten 200 Jahre, second, revised printing
© Bertz + Fischer GbR 2015
Translation © Alexander Locascio 2017

All rights reserved

The moral rights of the authors have been asserted

3 5 7 9 10 8 6 4 2

Verso
UK: 6 Meard Street, London W1F 0EG
US: 388 Atlantic Ave, Brooklyn, NY 11217
versobooks.com

Verso is the imprint of New Left Books

ISBN-13: 978-1-78478-614-4
ISBN-13: 978-1-78478-616-8 (US EBK)
ISBN-13: 978-1-78478-615-1(UK EBK)

British Library Cataloguing in Publication Data
A catalogue record for this book is
available from the British Library

Library of Congress Cataloging-in-Publication Data
A catalog record for this book is available
from the Library of Congress

Typeset in Sabon by MJ&N Gavan, Truro, Cornwall
Printed in the United States

Contents

CHAPTER I

Pikettymania

> For unto every one that hath shall be given, and he shall have
> abundance; but from him that hath not shall be taken away
> even that which he hath.
>
> (St Matthew 25:29)

The Gospel of St Matthew tells the story of a man who goes
abroad and leaves his fortune to his servants. He gives one
five talents of silver, he gives a second two talents and gives
a third one talent. The first two servants engage in trade and
double their silver. The third servant, however, buries his
talent. When the master returns, he praises the first two for
their faithfulness: 'Well done, thou good and faithful servant:
thou hast been faithful over a few things.' He accuses the
third of being an 'unprofitable', 'wicked and slothful servant',
and gives the order: 'take therefore the talent from him, and
give it unto him which hath ten talents'.

> For unto every one that hath shall be given, and he shall have
> abundance; but from him that hath not shall be taken away
> even that which he hath. (St Matthew 25: 28–29)

The 'Matthew Effect' is known not only in the field of sociol-
ogy. In the vernacular it is also known as '*Der Teufel scheißt
immer auf den größten Haufen*' (money makes money, literally: 'the devil always takes a shit on the biggest pile'); the
rich get richer; success leads to success; it always rains where
it's already wet. Nobody has ever got rich through hard work,

says another maxim, and an English saying points the way to the alternative: money makes money.

That which one can regard as either a suspicion or knowledge based upon experience was proved by the economist Thomas Piketty. At least, that is what he intended to do. In a huge book with vast quantities of statistical material – which, thanks to the expansion of the financial bureaucracy as a result of the bourgeois revolutions, deals primarily with the last 200 years – he depicts how, when and why the distribution of wealth has become, and is becoming, increasingly unequal.

When Piketty's book *Capital in the Twenty-First Century* was published in France in the summer of 2013, it had a friendly reception. However, it did not get very much attention.[1] The hype first began with the American edition in March 2014, when Paul Krugman, winner of the Nobel Prize in economics in 2008, celebrated Piketty's work as 'the most important book of the year – and possibly of the decade'. It was 'a book that will change both the way we think about society and the way we do economics'. Martin Wolf, columnist for the British *Financial Times*, declared it to be an 'extraordinarily important book' that nobody should ignore. The German economist and so-called '*Wirtschaftsweise*', or 'economic sage' Peter Bofinger praised the book and attested that Piketty had succeeded in finally putting the urgently necessary discussion about the future of the market economy at the centre of public attention.

An economist as rock star: Piketty as cover boy

For a long time, the book occupied the number one spot of the Amazon bestseller list, the first printing sold out quickly, and it is supposed to have made the author a millionaire. Piketty's first reading tour through the United States 'resembled that of a rock star'. He presented his findings to the United Nations, the International Monetary Fund (IMF) and the senior staff of US President Obama. Large newspapers in Europe and America devoted much space to the book and vied for interviews in which Piketty could elucidate and defend his theses. The only thing missing from the rock star comparison were tour dates on his website.

The hype is remarkable, since alongside the praise it was maintained that Piketty advanced a 'most simplistic thesis' and provided evidence in his book for 'that which the people have known for a long time'. And not just 'the people'; numerous empirical investigations in the past had demonstrated the divergence between rich and poor in the industrialized countries. So if Piketty was merely writing what was already well known and proven, what was all the excitement about? In order to explain that, one first has to consider the *context* in which the book was published. And then, one has to consider the *content* of the book.

CHAPTER 2

The Prelude: Redistribution, Inequality and Debt Crisis

The great attention that Piketty received can be explained for one thing by the contemporary economic situation and its pre-history. In the 1980s there began what was later called the 'neoliberal age'. Among other things, it involved the redistribution of the tax burden from capital income to wage income and consumption. The concept behind this was lifting the burden from capital in order to promote investments and thus economic growth.

Between states this became noticeable as a competition for investment, in which every country lowered its taxes on capital and business in order to attract capital. This strategy of 'courting capital' was regarded as without alternative, since businesses and investors would otherwise leave the country:

> Whoever keeps taxes high here shouldn't wonder if businesses move to countries that are more advantageous tax-wise. What use are nice theories if businesses close or move away? We cannot allow that under any circumstances. Germany must court enterprise capital, since only that guarantees innovations, growth, and jobs.[1]

Here are some examples of the consequences of this competition between states in Europe:

- Tax competition. Between 1997 and 2007, the average corporate tax rate in the old EU countries fell from 38 to 29 per cent, in the new EU entry countries from 32 to 19 per

cent. Cuts in corporate tax rates started as early as in the
1980s. Between 1980 and 2006 the average company tax
rate in the EU-15 (UK) fell from 49 (52) per cent to 30 (30)
per cent; for the EU-25 it was only 25 per cent in 2006.[2]
Eurostat: 'Finally, the EU has by and large become a low-tax
area when it comes to statutory corporate tax rates.'[3]

- At the same time the top personal income tax rate in the
EU-15 (UK) went down from an average of 67 (60) per
cent in 1980 to 48 (40) per cent in 2006. For the EU-25
it was only 42 per cent.[4] US President Reagan lowered the
top tax rate in 1982, initially from 70 per cent to 50 per
cent, and then to 28 per cent.

- Transition to dual income taxation. Profits on interest and
from dividends are increasingly subject to a flat tax and no
longer to an individual, progressive tax rate. That means
that the higher the income, the higher therefore the income
tax rate, the more the taxpayer profits from the flat tax
upon income from interest.

- A shift from direct to indirect taxation, primarily taxes
upon consumption. The main source is the value added tax
(VAT). According to EU regulations, the VAT can range
between 15 and 25 per cent. In the last few decades, the
rate has approached the upper limit. Thus, between 1980
and 2008 the VAT in Germany rose from 13 to 19 per
cent, in the UK from 15 to 17.5 per cent, in France from
17.6 to 19.6 per cent, and in Italy from 14 to 20 per cent.
In the course of the euro crisis, the VAT has been further
increased in many countries. Added to this are rising
so-called ecological taxes on energy. Taxes upon consumption disproportionately burden poorer households whose
income is spent primarily upon consumption.

- The tax burden on labour in the European Union started
growing strongly in the early 1970s and continued to grow.
The consequence: a shift in the tax burden. In 2007, within
the EU-27, consumption taxes have contributed a third of

the total revenue from taxes. Taxes upon employed labour income amount to about 40 per cent of the share. About one-fifth falls upon taxes on capital.

- Part of the competition between states to attract capital was, alongside tax policies, wage policy and the weakening of labour unions, whose negotiating position weakened on the basis of increasing unemployment and tangible repression against organized labour, particularly in the US and Britain. As a consequence, since the 1970s and 1980s, in every single industrial country the share of national income accounted for by wages declined.[5] The share of income from business activity and wealth rose accordingly. From the 1980s until the 2000s, the share of economic performance allotted to capital income rose by about 11.5 per cent in Germany, 18.7 per cent in Italy, by about 19.4 per cent in France and by about 18.7 per cent in Spain. In the United States and Britain, the increase was almost 8 per cent for both.

Declining taxes on capital, declining wages – the consequence was an increasingly unequal distribution of income and wealth. Since the 1980s on, the gap widened in almost all industrial countries.[6] Thus in the US, the share of total income of the wealthiest 5 per cent of households grew from 22 per cent to almost 34 per cent between 1983 and 2008.

This development, however, was not regarded as a scandal. It was usually explained as a consequence of 'globalization' (that is, the greater reservoir of labour available to business worldwide, which is to say increased competition between workers for jobs) and of 'technological change' that gave an advantage to highly skilled workers and exerted downward pressure on the income of low-skilled workers.[7] This growing inequality was thus regarded first of all as an inevitable consequence of 'globalization' and 'technology', and secondly as the result of the necessary and growth-promoting competition between countries for capital and investment. Inequality was positively regarded even within social democratic political parties as a spur to performance and thus an engine of growth.[8] According to the ideology, all would profit from this promotion of growth in accordance with the motto: a rising tide lifts all boats.

This legitimation of inequality encountered difficulties with the financial and economic crisis starting in 2008. The crisis incurred enormous costs – especially for the bank bailouts – which precipitated an increase in public debt. Between 2008 and 2013, the government gross debt for Euro states grew from 70 per cent to 93 per cent of economic output. In the UK, it increased from 52 to 91 per cent of economic output, in the US from 73 to 104 per cent, and even in Japan, where public debt was already at 192 per cent, it increased to 244 per cent.

This increase in public debt was essentially due to the financial crisis.[9] However, politicians and the majority of economists interpreted it as a problem of state expenditures under the mantra 'we've been living beyond our means'. Financial markets were not regarded as the source of the crisis; conversely, the slogan was put forward that through austerity policies, states would have to win back 'the trust of the markets'.

The consequence in many countries was a drastic reduction in expenditures and a search by states for new sources of revenue in order to decrease budget deficits. This put the question on the table: who should pay for the costs of the crisis and the bank bailouts? The value added tax was increased in many places, which made consumption more expensive. The crisis and austerity programmes led at the same time to a considerable decline in wages and social benefits. Largely spared, in contrast, were the banks, although they were simultaneously pilloried as the parties responsible for the crisis. The 'wealthiest' were also spared, this despite the fact that the share of the wealthiest per centile of the population of total pre-tax income in all industrial countries had risen for decades, thanks also to the developments that had ultimately led to the crisis.[10]

With the crisis it also became clear that it was not only public debt that had risen. The debt of private households and businesses had increased for decades. Thus total debt in the US (for both the public and private sector) amounted at the beginning of the 1980s to about 120 per cent of gross domestic product (GDP); but by 2008 it had risen to 240 per cent of GDP. In the eurozone, the ratio of total debt to GDP had risen from 150 to almost 300 per cent, in the UK from 150 to 280 per cent, and in Japan from 250 to almost 400 per cent.[11] These obligations on the part of debtors corresponded to the claims of creditors; it thus reflected the rise in private financial wealth.

Crisis, debt, growing inequality and enormous financial wealth – all of that called for an explanation and split the thinking of the economic mainstream, which had been rather unified before the crisis.[12] The still orthodox 'neoliberals' among these economists interpreted the crisis as a consequence of the failures of states, in particular of erroneous interest rate policy on the part of central banks. For others, in contrast, the crisis was a consequence of a liberalization of financial markets that had gone too far.

Alongside all this, in the years after the outbreak of the crisis, many scholars and institutions began to also discuss the growing gap between rich and poor as a cause of the crisis. What had earlier been the domain of leftists and critics of capitalism had reached the mainstream. The latter now problematized growing inequality; not, however, primarily as a social problem or a question of justice, but rather as a problem for the economic conjuncture and economic stability. It was pointed out that growing inequality was an important, if not the decisive, reason for the crisis of the financial system.

The upturn of the stock exchanges and a tendency towards the decreasing taxation of capital gains had supposedly led to a swelling of financial wealth which discharged in crisis. With a more just distribution of wealth and a stronger tax burden upon wealth, the state could thus contribute to making the economy and the financial system more stable. It could also create new sources of revenue in order to limit or decrease public debt.[13]

The following are a few examples of reconsideration by the mainstream:

- In November of 2010, the IMF published a working paper[14] that pointed out the connection between growing inequality and financial crises. Three years later, a similar paper followed.[15] Income inequality, warned the IMF, could lead to non-sustainable growth, since it is primarily the poorer strata of society that spend their money entirely on consumption. Through that, money flows back into economic circulation. In the period before the crisis, however, poorer households hardly achieved any growth in income. In order to increase or maintain their level of consumption, they often had to resort to credit. Thus, on the one hand, increasing inequality leads poorer households to take on excessive debt according to the IMF. On the other hand, the rich have gotten richer, and have not consumed this growth in income, but rather invested it, which is to say: lent it at interest. That has led, secondly, to a constantly increasing growth in the volume of investment capital. In the quest for profitable investments, capital has been thrown into increasingly risky forms of investment. The result: the wealthy accumulate more and more financial assets covered by loans to the poor, which increases the probability of financial crises.[16]
- In April 2011[17] and at the beginning of 2014,[18] the IMF upped the ante: in two investigations, the IMF came to

the conclusion that economic growth is more sustainable and stable in economies with a more equal distribution of wealth. In October 2013, the IMF considered a compulsory levy on all wealth in order to increase state revenues and decrease public debt.[19]

- In light of the crisis and inequality, the conservative journalist and Margaret Thatcher biographer Charles Moore admitted in July 2011 in the *Daily Telegraph*: 'I'm starting to think that the Left might actually be right.'[20] A month later, Moore was quoted approvingly by the then publisher of the *Frankfurter Allgemeine Zeitung* Frank Schirrmacher: 'It has been shown – as the left has always claimed – that a system that entered the stage to allow the advancement of many has become perverted into a system that enriches the few.'[21] Also in August 2011, the third-richest man in the world, Warren Buffett, demanded higher taxes for rich and super-rich Americans: 'My friends and I have been coddled long enough by a billionaire-friendly Congress.'[22]

- Between September and November 2011, the Occupy Wall Street movement occupied Zuccotti Park in the financial district of New York City. Their movement slogan: 'We are the 99%.' The intent was to protest the power of the richest 1 per cent of the population. Already in May 2011, the US Nobel Prize-winning economist Joseph E. Stiglitz had pointed out the problem in an article for *Vanity Fair* (its title, 'Of the 1%, by the 1%, for the 1%', was a reference to a phrase in Abraham Lincoln's Gettysburg Address: 'of the people, by the people, and for the people') and spoke to Occupy Wall Street. The most prominent member of the Occupy movement, however, is the American anthropologist David Graeber, whose book *Debt: The First 5000 Years* raised a storm in 2011 and like Piketty's book haunted the review pages – even if Graeber does not see himself as part of the mainstream. In addition, an above average number of journalistic and scholarly contributions on the topic of inequality were published – not just in Germany – sometimes with very different choices of focus and emphasis.[23]

- In November 2013, the new Pope Francis lamented in his first apostolic exhortation: 'While the earnings of a minority are growing exponentially, so too is the gap separating the majority from the prosperity enjoyed by those happy few. This imbalance is the result of ideologies which defend the absolute autonomy of the marketplace and financial speculation.'[24]

- In March 2014, the general secretary of the Organisation for Economic Co-operation and Development (OECD), José Ángel Gurría, said that 'urgent action' was 'needed to tackle rising inequality'.[25] In May he warned 'we underline the toll that ever-rising inequality takes on people's lives and the wider economy'.[26] Now other liberal institutions followed: 'More social justice creates at the same time more wealth and growth', wrote the Bertelsmann Stiftung,[27] and in June even a member of the European Central Bank disclosed that inequality could 'cause financial instability'.[28] Thus, the notion that just societies are better for all – which was greeted with smiles of approval in 2009 when Richard Wilkinson and Kate Pickett presented it in their book *The Spirit Level* – had reached the mainstream.

So, even before Thomas Piketty's book, the topic of 'inequality' had arrived in the economic mainstream, and with the following line of argumentation: inequality and poverty are no longer regarded so much as a consequence of capitalist economic growth, but rather as a brake on such growth and as a problem for stability. Despite the tendency to speak about this issue in moral terms, the central questions are economic ones: 'Would the U.S. economy be better off with a narrower income gap?' asks the rating agency S&P, and the OECD states: 'inequality hurts economic growth.'[29] What stands at the centre of attention are no longer the problems that the poor have with capitalism, but the problems that the poor pose for capitalism and its growth. The demand that follows from this is no longer a fundamental change of economic system, but merely a correction of the existing one – and not a correction of wealth to the benefit of the poor, but a correction of poverty for the benefit of wealth. The goal is not a better life for people – such a better life is only supposed to be a means of making economic growth smoother and faster. This chorus was joined by those who feared a dissolution of 'social peace' (in Germany, for example) by the evocation of 'American conditions'.

CHAPTER 3

The Book

The subject of income and wealth inequality has been Piketty's topic for many years. That is why he could write right at the beginning of his new book: 'This book is based on fifteen years of research (1998–2013) devoted essentially to understanding the historical dynamics of wealth and income.'[1] With that, Piketty's guiding question is outlined: how do wealth and income develop long-term, and what are the driving forces of this development? The book is structured according to this question. It consists of four large sections:

- Income and Capital (p. 39ff)
- The Dynamics of the Capital/Income Ratio (p. 113ff)
- The Structure of Inequality (p. 237ff)
- Regulating Capital in the Twenty-First Century (p. 237ff)

In the first section, Piketty introduces the reader to the topic and discusses what capital and income are and how they can be measured. He then comes to the actual topic of the book: how does the relationship between wealth on the one hand and income (income from labour and earnings on capital) on the other hand develop in the long run? And why? What patterns can be recognized? Finally, Piketty ventures a prognosis about how the relation between wealth and income will develop, and on this basis he makes economic policy proposals for how the world could improve.

Where does Piketty get his data?

Piketty's data set, which has been much praised, is based inter alia upon tax records that he and his research partners have sifted through and processed over the last few years. On the one hand, Piketty is surprised that this material has not been used previously, but at the same time provides an explanation: the statistical study of tax records is an 'academic no-man's-land, too historical for economists and too economistic for historians'.[2] That is surprising to the extent that tax records first make it possible to take a long-term analytical perspective.[3] Most of Piketty's data series thus begin with the twentieth century, when many Western industrial countries first implemented an income tax. More difficult than in the case of income is the data for income from wealth and the size of wealth. Whereas income is well documented by tax authorities, wealth is not.[4] Piketty notes: 'I trust the quantification of wealth for the year 1913 more than that of 2013. National income is recorded relatively well, but the distribution of income up to the highest tiers is another question.'[5]

The most important source for the book is the World Top Incomes Database (WTID), the result of cooperation between thirty scholars and many research institutes, which Piketty helped to build in the last ten years.[6] The database now encompasses more than twenty countries and is constantly updated. The first evaluations of the data had already been published in 2007 and 2010.

Partially to make his book more readable, Piketty did without a comprehensive data annex. In the book, one finds almost exclusively graphics that more or less vividly depict the developments described. However, the 'specialist audience' has the possibility of scrutinizing the data material: Piketty has put all of it on the internet.[7] The charts and illustrations featured or mentioned in the present book are also freely available as PDF files.[8]

At the centre: the ratio of capital to wealth and income to economic performance

At the centre of Piketty's analysis is the capital–income ratio. Of what is it comprised?

- National income (or income for short) is defined 'as the sum of all income available to the residents of a given country in a given year, regardless of the legal classification of that income'.[9]
- Capital, on the other hand, is defined 'as the sum total of nonhuman assets that can be owned and exchanged on some market'.[10] Under the term 'capital', Piketty subsumes all forms of real estate property (including owner-occupied housing) as well as finance capital and 'professional' wealth (factories, machines, infrastructure, patents, etc.) that is used by businesses or state agencies. Not 'human capital', however, since it can neither be owned by another person nor traded on the market. Piketty uses the terms 'capital' and 'wealth' synonymously,[11] and we will do so as well when describing his account.[12]

The two magnitudes capital and income provide the first and most important magnitude that Piketty works with: the capital–income ratio, abbreviated with the Greek letter β (beta). With this ratio, according to Piketty, inequality can be adequately examined over longer periods of time and depicted in a meaningful number. If, for example, the per capita wealth in a certain year amounts to 150,000 euro, and the annual average per capita income amounts to 30,000 euro, then wealth is five times income. The capital–income ratio is thus 5 (since 150,000:30,000 = 5). According to Piketty, the capital–income ratio in the Western industrial countries is at the moment actually between 5 and 6. However, both wealth as well as income change with the passage of time. Depending upon the direction in which the magnitudes change, the capital–income ratio becomes larger or smaller. Income on the one hand comprises income that comes from labour, such as wages, salaries or fees, and on the other hand by capital income such as profits, interest, rents and dividends that are all based in property in the form of means of production, real estate or securities.

Wealth grows when part of income is not consumed, but saved, which is to say used in order to increase a pool of wealth, for example by purchasing securities or real estate. It goes without saying that the only people who can build up or increase wealth are those who do not live hand-to-mouth, or who have rich parents – that is, who increase their wealth through inheritance. If the magnitudes capital and income grow unequally, the capital–income ratio β changes. Potentially, the inequality tracked by Piketty also increases.

Returns on capital and growth: r > g

What influences the movement of wealth and income? According to Piketty, the pool of wealth tends to increase more quickly than income, so that the capital–income ratio increases. Piketty says the reason for this is that returns on capital (usually abbreviated as 'r') are in terms of historical average much greater than the growth of economic performance or of income ('g' for 'growth').

Why is that the case? What influences the growth of wealth (r) on the one hand and economic growth (g) on the other?

- Growth of economic performance/income (g) is, according to Piketty, essentially dependent upon the development of the (working) population and upon technological progress.
- The rate of growth of wealth (r) in contrast depends strongly upon the risk that the owners of wealth are exposed to with their investments. The rate of growth

of r changes with the form of investment and the degree of speculation connected with it: the higher the risk, the greater r is. Thus, on average, according to Piketty, riskier stock investments or other forms of shareholding yield relatively high returns of 7 to 8 per cent. Real estate, in contrast, yields returns of only 3 to 4 per cent. Savings and checking accounts pay interest on saved money at the moment with rates of barely more than 2 per cent.

Piketty comes to the conclusion that the yearly return on capital r – despite all fluctuations and differences – averages out over the long term at about 4 to 5 per cent. The long-term rate of growth of economic performance g in contrast averages out at 1 to 2 per cent, and is therefore much smaller than the return on capital. Piketty expresses this in a formula: $r > g$.

So, income grows slower than wealth. This fact alone, however, does not yet automatically mean that inequality also increases. The reason: if all people owned an equal amount of wealth, all of them would equally profit from a strong growth of capital. In fact, however, wealth is unequally distributed, according to Piketty. He does not explain why that is. Rather, he assumes inequality as a given, and examines its development over time. This demonstrates, according to Piketty, that the strong growth of wealth in contrast to that of income exacerbates an inequality characteristic of all societies: those who have, receive (more). The rich become richer. According to Piketty, increasingly inequality is not a coincidence, but rather inscribed into economic development. Piketty says this is the case not only under capitalism, but also in other economic forms. However, Piketty does not wish for this diagnosis of growing inequality to be understood as a call to class struggle: 'To be clear, my purpose here is not to plead the case of workers against owners but rather to gain as clear as possible a view of reality.'[13]

Historical reconstruction: how inequality has developed

After the 'explanation' of growing inequality, Piketty turns to the history of inequality and the capital–income ratio: according to his calculations, the ratio r > g has been valid for the last 2,000 years. Before the assertion of capitalist relations, there was de facto no economic growth. Therefore, g tended to stand at zero until about the year 1700, and r was thus correspondingly larger.[14] Why was g so low? Because, before the eighteenth century, there was no noteworthy technological progress. According to Piketty, economic growth was thus based solely upon population growth, and per capita growth of income was therefore zero. It was first around the year 1500 that growth slowly set in; it then developed abruptly with the beginning of industrialization and made a further great leap forward in 1913, on the threshold of world war. Up to then, according to Piketty, r was between 4 and 5 per cent, so r > g. However, for the period before the eighteenth century, Piketty has hardly any reliable material. Even for the eighteenth century, he draws upon information from novels.

The capital–income ratio now dominant in Western industrial countries is almost as high as that on the eve of the First World War. For Piketty, this phase before the First World War and the present characterizes the extremes of the long-term development of the capital–income ratio so far.

- In France and Britain, the capital–income ratio between 1700 and 1910 amounted to about 7, then fell until 1950 to about 2.5 in Britain and less than 3 in France. After that, it rose again and approached a value of 5 in Britain and almost 6 in France in the year 2010.
- In the US, things looked similar, even if the ratio was initially low and only rose to 5 until 1910. Then it fell rapidly, ultimately stabilized between 5 and 5.5, and fell again after 1929 to 4 (in the year 1950). Only from the 1980s did inequality in the US increase again, and in 2010 reached

about 4.5 – with a tendential rise. The inequality curve in the industrial countries accordingly takes the form of a 'U', whereby 1913 and the present constitute the peaks so far for the Western industrial countries.[15]

How capital has changed

According to Piketty, in the last 200 years, not only has the capital–income ratio changed, but also the forms in which capital exists. The eighteenth and nineteenth centuries were not yet characterized by industrial capital. Back then, wealth existed primarily in the form of farmland and government bonds. Thus agricultural land was one of the most important investments for capital until the nineteenth century and yielded a ground rent between 4 and 5 per cent. Taxes and inflation were low, which made public bonds an important form of investment for regular income. Moreover, we know from novels or biographies of various figures that, during this period, inheritances were central for building wealth, among other things in order to pursue certain life paths. Not infrequently, some waited with longing for their inheritances to come due. At this point, Piketty could have quoted the penniless Karl Marx, who wrote in 1852 to his friend Friedrich Engels concerning his uncle: 'If the cur dies now I shall be out of this pickle.' Marx was hoping for an inheritance after he had come up 'empty' after the death of his father. Engels replied to Marx: 'My congratulations on the news of the illness of the old Brunswick inheritance-thwarter; I trust the catastrophe will at last come to pass.'[16]

With growing productivity, fewer people on a smaller area can produce more agricultural and silvicultural goods. Fewer people were involved in agriculture. Piketty traces how agricultural land declined in significance compared to other asset investments. In France as well as in Britain, wealth in the form of agricultural land (in relation to income) was most relevant, but declined radically up to 1900, and today ekes out a rather

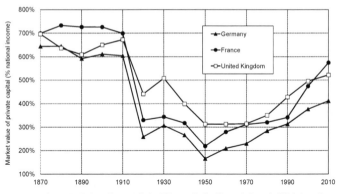

Aggregate private wealth was worth about 6-7 years of national income in Europe in 1910, between 2 and 3 years in 1950, and between 4 and 6 years in 2010. Sources and series: see piketty.pse.ens.fr/capital21c.

Figure 3.1. The capital–income ratio in Europe, 1870–2010

insignificant existence. With urbanization, the importance of land as capital increased, but now primarily in the form of real estate wealth.[17] Particularly from the 1970s onward, real estate played a greater role again. This became clear in light of the real estate price bubble in Japan (in the 1980s) and in the US, Spain, Ireland and the Netherlands in the 2000s. The bursting of the latter bubbles triggered the most recent global financial crisis. Piketty summarizes: 'Over the long run, the nature of wealth was totally transformed: capital in the form of agricultural land was gradually replaced by industrial and financial capital and urban real estate.'[18]

The nineteenth century was still characterized by extreme inequality – primarily in France and in Paris, where most wealth was concentrated. The wealthiest 10 per cent possessed up to 85 per cent of all wealth – an inequality that intensified up to the end of the century. Thus the French Revolution did not contribute to a 'democratization' of the relations of wealth. In Britain, development took a similar form.[19]

Germany is more or less comparable to France and the UK. In light of the relatively long-lasting relevance of farm

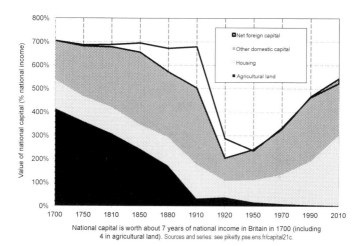

Figure 3.2. Capital in Britain, 1700–2010

land as wealth, it is more similar to France. However, a big difference was the smaller share in wealth abroad on the eve of the First World War – Germany was simply not an important colonial power.

Compared to these numbers, the US was definitely more egalitarian. The richest 1 per cent of the population did not possess 40 per cent of the total wealth; up to the beginning of the nineteenth century, the capital–income ratio in the United States amounted to only about 3; only in 1913 did the capital–income ratio climb to 5.

The great redistribution through the world wars and stock market crash

Before 1914, in all important industrial countries the capital–income ratio had undergone an extremely strong rise. Only a few years afterwards, however, it underwent a drastic reduction. One reason for this was of course the loss of wealth in the form of 'war damages'. A further reason was the devaluation of financial wealth in the form of government bonds: government bonds were already held in the eighteenth and nineteenth centuries, but in the course of war financing from 1914 on, their importance increased. After the First World War, these assets were devalued by inflation. In order to minimize the effects of inflation upon the general public and curb the price spiral, rent controls were also introduced, which reduced the returns on real estate. And finally, in their financial need, governments decided upon higher taxes upon inheritance and top incomes, which further eroded wealth – at least in France, Germany, Britain and the US.[20]

This taxation was something new. Before the war 'tax rates, even on the most astronomical incomes, remained extremely low ... This was true everywhere, without exception.'[21]

In France, the top tax rate – which was only valid anyway for a tiny minority of taxpayers – was at about 2 per cent. First in the radically changed political and financial environment after the war were the top tax rates raised to 'modern' levels: to 50 per cent in the year 1920, to 60 per cent in 1924, and even to 72 per cent a year later. During the period of peace before the First World War, 'tax rates were never raised significantly. In Prussia, the top rate remained stable at 3 per cent from 1891 to 1914 and then rose to 4 per cent from 1915 to 1918, before ultimately shooting up to 40 per cent in 1919–1920, in a radically changed political climate.'[22] Developments were rather similar in the US and Britain, where very low top tax rates were also drastically increased after the First World War; in the US to 77 per cent and in Britain to 40 per cent.

The First World War provided for a somewhat more equal distribution of wealth, but it was followed almost seamlessly by the boom of the 'roaring twenties', in which inequality achieved new records. The boom had its sudden end in 1929, when the stock market crash initiated what is still the severest world economic crisis ever. In this crash, not only were assets like stocks and bonds devalued, but the crisis also shattered the world market, which was already well developed by

1913: trade and production collapsed worldwide. Increasing unemployment also put pressure upon wages, but not to the same extent as asset values. In the US, the government under President Roosevelt pursued policies in the 1930s that led to a considerable shift of the capital–income ratio at the cost of wealth. After the Second World War, which further decimated wealth, these policies were implemented in other countries. The result: the capital–income ratio, which had been at 6 or 7 in Europe before 1914, declined until 1950 to 2 or 3. In the US, which was not affected to the same extent by the destruction of wealth by the war, it fell from 5 to 3.5.

The lessons of the Second World War and the Superpower Bloc confrontation

The great crisis from 1929 was first politically overcome after 1945: a global currency system of fixed exchange rates was established; in many industrial countries, the movement of capital was strongly regulated; wealth and high incomes were strongly taxed; and many economic sectors were withdrawn from the logic of profit through the act of nationalization. Thus, Piketty refers to the example of France on the basis of nationalizations that occurred after 1945 as a 'capitalism without capitalists', since many key businesses and the banking sector were dominated by the state. The concentration of wealth as well as income from wealth in France has, according to Piketty, never really recovered from the shock of 1914 to 1945. Between 1910 and 1920, the richest tenth of French households held 90 per cent of total wealth. Between 1950 and 1970, this share supposedly fell to 'only' 60 to 70 per cent. In the same time period, the share of wealth of the richest hundredth fell from 60 to 20–30 per cent.

'The available data for the other European countries confirm that this has been a general phenomenon. In Britain, the upper decile's share fell from more than 90 per cent on the eve of World War I to 60–65 per cent in the 1970s; it is currently around 70 per cent. The top centile's share collapsed in the wake of the twentieth century's shocks, falling from nearly 70 per cent in 1910–1920 to barely more than 20 per cent in 1970–1980, then rising to 25–30 per cent today.'[23] Things looked similar in the United States.

Hidden behind these pure numbers, however, are radical changes within society. According to Piketty, states used their tax revenues in order to build welfare state structures. With the loss of significance of the super-rich, and a new relation between the state and the market, a new middle class emerged that could build up wealth by means of its labour-power and income. The emergence of this middle class was the result of the decline of the capital–income ratio. 'In every case, we find that what the wealthiest 10 per cent lost mainly benefited the "patrimonial middle class" (defined as the middle 40 per cent of the wealth hierarchy) and did not go to the poorest half of the population, whose share of total wealth has always been minuscule (generally around 5 per cent), even in Sweden (where it was never more than 10 per cent).'[24]

Wealth and inheritance were thus no longer the only roads to prosperity. Asset accumulation had been 'democratized'. With that, according to Piketty, in the era between the 1950s and 1970s a central bourgeois promise had been redeemed: hard work paid off – thanks to the real possibility of social mobility on the basis of an expanded education system, social insurance systems, a progressive income tax, and a high tax burden on large fortunes. 'During the decades that followed World War II, inherited wealth lost much of its importance, and for the first time in history, perhaps, work and study became the surest routes to the top.' The inequality that still persisted could therefore be legitimized as a consequence of different capabilities: 'democratic modernity is founded on the belief that inequalities based on individual talent and effort are more justified than other inequalities.'[25]

Like many studies critical of capitalism, Piketty also emphasizes that, between the end of the Second World War and the crisis from the middle/end of the 1970s, a special era reigned that is sometimes referred to ironically as a 'golden age' or 'the brief dream of eternal prosperity': rising wages, the increasing significance of the middle class, taxes upon high incomes and fortunes and the expansion of the welfare state did not stand in opposition to a dynamic development of the economy. Between 1950 and 1970, the economy grew on average annually about 2.3 per cent (US) and 4 per cent (in Western Europe). This era ended with the global economic crisis of 1973, which was also a turning point in the development of the capital–income ratio. With the crisis, the political climate in the US and Britain also changed. In both countries, new policies were pursued from the end of the 1970s onward that spread to many other countries and which still persist today: the era of neoliberalism was inaugurated. In this context, Piketty speaks of a resurgence of capital and of the emergence of a class of super-rich.[26]

The resurgence of capital and the class of the super-rich

The crisis of the 1970s was expressed in shrinking economic performance and a high rate of inflation. The US and Britain reacted first to this situation: they deregulated the markets – above all capital and labour markets – liberalized commodity and service markets, and privatized large swathes of state property, by which capital was able to annex new spheres of growth. In addition, there was a radical reversal in taxation: 'After experiencing a great passion for equality from the 1930s through the 1970s, the United States and Britain veered off with equal enthusiasm in the opposite direction.'[27] Over the last three decades, their top tax rates fell far under the levels of those of, for example, France and Germany. There, the top tax rates remained under 60 per cent between 1930 and 1940, never went over 70 per cent even after 1950, and only fell slightly from the 1980s on. In both Anglo-Saxon countries, in contrast, the drop height was considerably greater. Between 1940 and the end of the 1970s, the top tax rate in Britain was always above 90 per cent, in the US between 70 and 95 per cent. With the tax reform of 1986 under Ronald Reagan, the top tax rate in the US reached a low point of 28 per cent; developments were similar under Margaret Thatcher.[28]

Changes in tax policy shifted the capital–income ratio to the advantage of capital. But additional forces were also pulling in the same direction:

- As Piketty shows, there had always been an important difference between public and private wealth.[29] Since the 1970s, however, one can observe a widening gap in all G8 states: private wealth is increasing in relation to public wealth, and that makes possible the accumulation of additional private wealth.
- This development was accompanied by a loss of significance of the wage. Since the 1980s, the wage share – the share of wages in national income – has had a tendency to decline in almost all industrial countries. Inversely, the share of income from wealth and business activity has increased.[30]
- But income disparity has also increased: whereas real wages stagnated or even declined for the majority of employees, the top tier of the income hierarchy earned incomparably more, which contributed to the fact that top earners, thanks to their incomes, where able to increase their wealth. After the Second World War until the neoliberal turn, the 10 per cent of top earners were never able to command more than 30 per cent of all income. That was the case for both Europe as well as the US, where, from the 1970s on, inequality increased radically and the upper tenth in the meantime earned more than 45 per cent

of all income. In the US, inequality of historical dimensions thus reigns; in Europe, income disparity has reached the level of that before the Second World War.[31]

- In order to cut state expenditures and create 'incentives to work' for the unemployed, the welfare state, which for a long time was supposed to guarantee social mobility independent of the wage, was dismantled step by step.

- Prices for securities increased in the course of a growing financial market from the 1970s on, and increased (above all in the US and Britain) the proportion of wealth vis-à-vis income from labour.[32]

- While, empirically, returns on capital are stabilizing at over 4 per cent (after being at over 5 per cent between 1820 and 2012), according to Piketty growth (g) will develop in a weak manner. The above average economic growth after 1945 came to an end in the 1970s, and has since then 'normalized' in the US, but also in Western Europe, even if some parts of the world (China and India, for example) are still realizing high rates of growth. Against this background, Piketty is confronted with a similar 'logical contradiction'[33] supposedly also recognized by Marx with his theory of the tendency of the rate of profit to fall: on the one hand, returns on capital must decline (on the basis of a surplus of capital relative to possibilities for increasing productivity and hence returns on capital); on the other hand, on the basis of the growth in wealth, the power of rentiers has also increased, who maintain their claims upon an increasing share of economic growth (g), which in turn, however, can barely increase due to the blockade outlined above (surplus of capital). Thus returns on capital decrease in importance as a means of generating wealth in favour of inheritance.

The result of this trend is that, while the capital–income ratio was still at about 3.5 in the US in 1945, it has now risen to

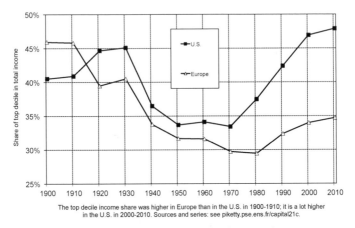

The top decile income share was higher in Europe than in the U.S. in 1900-1910; it is a lot higher in the U.S. in 2000-2010. Sources and series: see piketty.pse.ens.fr/capital21c.

Figure 3.3. Income inequality: Europe vs. the United States, 1900–2010

almost 5. Things look similar in Britain (5.5), France (6) and Germany (above 4). The concentration of wealth has thus increased.

Subsequently, inheritance as a source of wealth once again increased in importance. Piketty made that clear in an interview with the *Süddeutsche Zeitung* using the example of so-called generational justice: 'Europe is saying that we're leaving so much debt behind for our children. But the truth is that we're leaving them more wealth than any other generation before […] Prosperity is not properly distributed.'[34]

That which according to Piketty once allowed social mobility thanks to the welfare state, in contrast, is losing importance: economic performance and education. The latter has become devalued over the last few years: 'a high school diploma now represents what a grade school certificate used to mean, a college degree what a high school diploma used to stand for, and so on.'[35] At the same time, elite universities increased in importance. The educational system took on a selective function, rather than permitting social mobility independent of social background. This was the case not only in the US: 'It would be wrong, however, to imagine that unequal access to higher education is a problem solely in the United States. It is one of the most important problems that social states everywhere must face in the twenty-first century. To date, no country has come up with a truly satisfactory response.'[36]

A particular phenomenon since the 1980s has been that of a class of super-managers (only in the Anglo-Saxon countries, however).[37] With growing wage inequality a new wealthy elite arose, the so-called super-rich. Not only did the total number of billionaires increase. Total wealth also again became concentrated in the hands of a smaller group, albeit not as strongly as before 1913. The richest 10 per cent of US households owned 70 per cent of the total wealth, whereby half of the total belongs solely to the richest 1 per cent. The next 40 per cent, which Piketty identifies as the so-called middle class, owns only one-quarter of wealth – in the US, most of that is real estate. Almost nothing (5 per cent) remains for the remaining half of the total population. European societies, in comparison, are only a little bit more egalitarian, since there the richest 1 per cent owns 25 per cent of wealth and the middle class owns 35 per cent.

Piketty's forecast: inheritance instead of economic performance

Piketty foresees the continuation of this development of wealth, income and inequality in the near and distant future. He argues that returns on wealth (r) will continue to outpace the growth of income (g) on the basis of the weak development of g.

> With an average return on capital of 4–5 per cent, it is there-fore likely that r > g will again become the norm in the twenty-first century, as it had been throughout history until the eve of World War I. In the twentieth century, it took two

world wars to wipe away the past and significantly reduce the return on capital, thereby creating the illusion that the fundamental structural contradiction of capitalism (r > g) had been overcome.[38]

On the basis of his data, Piketty assumes that worldwide economic growth will level off on average between 1 and 2 per cent until the year 2100 and that r in contrast will level off at 4 to 5 per cent within the framework of the long-term trend. The ratio of r > g projected eighty years into the future has as a consequence, according to Piketty, a further redistribution of wealth and an acceleration of inequality.[39]

Piketty's look ahead into the future is therefore almost like a glance in its historical reflection. The composition of wealth might have changed – less land ownership, more financial and industrial capital – and the concentration of wealth is not as extreme as it was 100 years ago. Nonetheless, a trend highlights the devastating consequences of which Piketty warns against: the increase in importance of inheritance as a source of wealth, and the decrease in importance of 'economic performance' as a source of income. To take the example of France: between 1820 and 1900, inheritances reached a value that encompassed 16 to 25 per cent of national income. Between 1920 and 1940, this ratio declined and never went over 11 per cent. Until 1980, it declined to 3–7 per cent. After that, however, the inheritance party took off: in the meantime, the share of inheritances of national income is again almost at 16 per cent.

Things look similar in other countries.[40] What also rose at the same time was the share of endowments before death, that is to say 'early inheritances'. The consequences for the amassing of wealth are devastating, according to Piketty. Whereas, in 1970, the cumulative value of inherited wealth constituted about 45 per cent of total wealth, the share increased to about 60 per cent in the middle of the 1990s, and is tending

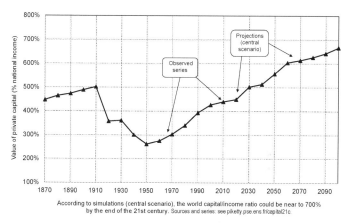

According to simulations (central scenario), the world capital/income ratio could be near to 700% by the end of the 21st century. Sources and series: see piketty.pse.ens.fr/capital21c.

Figure 3.4. The world capital–income ratio, 1870–2100

towards (depending upon the simulation) 80 or 90 per cent beginning in the year 2030.[41]

Thus there is the solidification and strengthening of a trend that leads to the constitution of a tiny elite. It is accompanied by the reorganization of the welfare state, in which for example the education system leads to a further homogenization of social milieus and does not at all make social mobility possible: the rich can afford the good schools and training, therefore obtaining the 'good jobs'. In contrast, the poor are denied this mobility. The relationships formed in the early stages of life, which ultimately lead to weddings, in turn constitute the basis for inheritances leading to a further intensification of the relations of wealth. The rich marry the rich, thus remaining among themselves, and inherit each other's growing wealth.

Why does Piketty refer to this trend as devastating? Here, we come to his central point of criticism of growing inequality. Let us recall: according to Piketty, in the phase of the 1950s to the 1970s, the central bourgeois promise – that effort is rewarded – was redeemed. Modern societies were based upon the assumption of the equality of individuals.

Material inequality could thus only be explained in terms of the inequality in the abilities of individuals.

In the future, however, says Piketty, it is not so much effort that will determine prosperity, but rather background and family, that is to say: inheritance. According to Piketty, Western societies are moving towards a state of affairs in which those who receive their wealth in the cradle 'call the shots'. Piketty refers to rentiers – that is, those whose income consists essentially of yields from property – as enemies of democracy.[42]

Piketty's central point of critique is aimed at the legitimation of inequality. Bourgeois society's self-description, in which inequality is a consequence of different abilities, will no longer be accurate in the future. To make a long story short: effort will no longer be worth it.

Piketty's contrast of pre- and post-tax returns up to the year 2010[43] already indicates the instrument with which he would like to set r > g right: with taxation.

What is to be done in the twenty-first century?

The absence of legitimation for unequal relations of wealth is reason enough for Piketty to change them. He does not regard it as acceptable that Western industrial societies are steering towards relations of distribution reminiscent of those on the eve of the First World War or during the Belle Époque. Instead of income, wealth based upon inheritance dominates; instead of effort, background dominates; the guarantee of prosperity is having the right relatives, not hard work. 'From this analysis I must now try to draw lessons for the future,' Piketty writes.[44] But how can the wheel of distribution be turned back? From Piketty's study, it is clear that it has mostly been crises, wars and accompanying tax policy that have lowered the capital–income ratio. But neither crises nor war are politically desired – thus taxing large wealth remains as an option. For Piketty, 'A tax on capital would promote the general interest over private interests while preserving economic openness and the forces of competition.'[45] The crisis of 2008 has occasionally led in Piketty's view to pragmatic economic policies, but has not initiated a fundamental correction.

According to Piketty, the 'second fiscal revolution' after 1945 – a broad and progressive taxation of income – first made possible the establishment of a welfare state. Piketty sees this as the guarantor for balanced relations of wealth[46]: 'in other words, the growth of the fiscal state over the last century basically reflects the constitution of a social state.'[47]

What Piketty has in mind as a political perspective is thus a defence and further development of a welfare state model. Taxation which makes welfare state benefits possible is a precondition for being able to guarantee public services as rights to which all are entitled. In this context, Piketty refers to the US Declaration of Independence of 1776, and the right famously articulated in its preamble of 'the pursuit of happiness' as well as to the Declaration of the Rights of Man and of the Citizen (*Déclaration des droits de l'homme et du citoyen*) proclaimed in France in 1789. Against this background, according to Piketty there is no stable argument as to why societies should not enact higher taxes – just as long as they are transparently and democratically legitimated. That is why Piketty's Chapter 14 is titled 'Rethinking the Progressive Income Tax'. Income taxes, along with taxes upon wealth and inheritances, are for Piketty the central starting point of shaping the relations of wealth in a more balanced way. This would also require 'new instruments', such as a progressive global tax on capital, which he refers to as 'a useful utopia'.[48]

The progressive tax on capital is a tax based upon the level of a fortune. But where do fortunes start? In an interview with the *Süddeutsche Zeitung*[49] Piketty says the tax should 'not affect the people who are just starting to amass wealth.

But as soon as somebody has crossed a certain threshold, they have to pay.' Where exactly this threshold should be, Piketty does not want to carve into stone. So he merely provides a few suggestions for discussion:

- In the case of a fortune of less than 1 million euros, there should be no taxes due. In the case of a fortune between 1 and 5 million euros, in contrast, there should be a tax of 1 per cent, and 2 per cent for anything over that, while 5 to 10 per cent should be the tax rate for hundreds of millions or more.[50]
- However, Piketty is not so sure, and also runs through other models, in which already in the case of a small fortune of 200,000 euros, a tax rate of 0.1 per cent is due.[51]
- The return on capital is, according to Piketty, a good criterion for taxation (and not just the size of a fortune), which is why he proposes using the average return of the previous year as a benchmark. In the case of an annual average return of 6 to 7 per cent, it would be entirely appropriate to tax fortunes of over 100 million euros at over 2 (up to 6) per cent.

Piketty thus does not propose any theoretically grounded level of taxation, but rather points out the necessity of a democratic debate concerning the question of what is 'appropriate'. Instead of arguing with theoretical statements, he argues historically and responds to the expected criticism: 'Historical experience shows, moreover, that such immense inequalities of wealth have little to do with the entrepreneurial spirit and are of no use in promoting growth.'[52]

In addition to wealth, in the future high incomes should also be taxed more strongly. Top earners should have to reckon with an income tax of up to 80 per cent. Such tax rates were not rare in history.[53] A progressive income tax with high taxation of top incomes should therefore be implementable in a democracy that takes its own principles seriously, according to Piketty.

Piketty is quite clear about the fact that businesses and the wealthy can get around taxes. It is also clear to him that states that make laws also try to attract capital with the lowest possible taxes. The problem here is the tax competition between states. Piketty wants to oppose this with international cooperation, which would be possible primarily within the framework of the EU.[54] Important for this would be the automatic exchange of banking information.[55] But at the same time, Piketty also admits self-critically that in order to avoid providing any loopholes to the wealthy, an unrealistically close cooperation between states for the implementation of a global tax would be necessary.

CHAPTER 4

Hype and Critique

Piketty's book, 685 pages thick in its English translation, caused a stir in the United States and Europe among economic and political elites (even if it is obvious that hardly anyone actually read the overflowing work all the way to the end).[1] But the hype was also joined by critique.

The Hype

Why did this book cause such a sensation, when so many studies, books, and more easily accessible texts on the topic had already been published? Multiple aspects serve to explain the hype:

- As already mentioned, the financial and economic crisis had called into question the legitimacy of the previously dominant dogma of freedom for capital, tax cuts and economic competitiveness. Furthermore, due to precarious state finances, the question of distribution was raised again; that is, the question as to who should bear the costs of stabilization. Both points led to contradictory positions among political and economic elites regarding the taxation of capital income and wealth.
- Furthermore, Piketty empirically proved, with enormous statistical effort and an apparent political neutrality, the folk wisdom that 'those who have, get': 'numbers never lie', it is often said. The book is not written by 'the latest "thinker" but a respected academic economist with real

numbers to go with his theory. We hadn't had anything like that in ages', enthused even an investment banker.[2] On the basis of his position as a university professor, Piketty also does not stand under suspicion of following certain interests – as would be the case, for example, with the IMF or trade unions.

Against this background, Piketty's thesis – that the tendency towards growing inequality is not a dumb coincidence but rather a law immanent to the economy or at least a strong tendency – is provocative. This statement is provocative because, if it is true, it would be necessary to take political countermeasures, which in turn would include a discussion about how this should happen. Piketty has made a few proposals in this regard, which not everyone likes – especially those at whose expense they would be made (the wealthy) and those whose economic policy doctrines contradict such tax policy intentions.

- For that reason, in the debate about Piketty, one also heard from those who saw themselves forced to react in order to insure that Piketty's proposals were not taken seriously by political decision-makers. Their conclusion can be summarized as follows: the admittedly true phenomenon of inequality cannot be dealt with by 'the wrong people'. Ultimately, they claim, the same failure cannot be made as in the 1960s, when the debate about justice was left to 'false prophets' that many citizens wanted to follow into the 'socialist land of milk and honey'. That is what Stephan Werhahn, national chair of the Small- and Medium-sized Business Association of the German CDU/CSU, as well as a delegate of the Association of Catholic Businessmen, says in his preface to an engagement with Piketty's work.[3] When even convinced opponents of Piketty's tax policy demands are forced to react to Piketty, something happens that they would rather avoid: a widespread public discussion about Piketty and his theses.

- The statement mentioned above – that inequality becomes subject to the pressure of social legitimation and is also bad for the economy – has led to a debate among social elites, which is carried out inter alia in the op-ed pages (see for example Frank Schirrmacher, Charles Moore, et al.). Among sections of the US liberal bourgeoisie, there was even a proper campaign to discuss Piketty – led by Paul Krugman, who as a Keynesian is hardly on Piketty's wavelength in terms of economic theory (we will return to this point shortly). In the print edition of the *New York Times*, Piketty has been mentioned in almost 100 articles since the book's publication. Paul Krugman blogged almost daily about the topic, and to kick things off wrote extensively and prominently about Piketty in the *New York Review of Books*.[4] The fact, however, that a discussion about the correct social and economic policy course is being conducted among elites, sometimes quite heatedly, points to a split between an old 'orthodoxy' and those demanding a moderate turnaround, and offers a completely different sounding board for a book like *Capital in the Twenty-First Century* than the Occupy movement or the dissatisfaction of trade unions over the fact that their power to negotiate has declined. If social elites had discussed other books in a similar manner, those books would have surely also experienced hype that no social movement could have generated. Nonetheless, it needs to be explained why there are no reservations about engaging with Piketty's book, which raises the final point.

- While Piketty attacks the dominant economic form, capitalism, he never argues in an anti-capitalist way. First of all, his 'laws of distribution' according to his work are valid in every economic formation, not just in capitalism (which he also leaves conceptually vague). For Piketty, growing inequality is a law of wealth per se, not of a specifically capitalist form of wealth. Secondly, his political demands do not amount to a fundamental transformation of the system, but rather are limited to a few changes in the tax system, which are supposed to make capitalism more stable. Piketty's enormously constructive critique of capitalism makes him compatible to the reigning crisis discourse. Despite all coquetry, Piketty never misses a chance to distance himself from Marx's ideas (which are attributed to him).

There are thus more reasons for the extraordinary success of the book than 'the right timing', the 'personal charisma' of the author, and an 'easily understood "world formula"'.[5]

Critique
So much for the hype and the explanation for it. Piketty did not just receive undivided agreement, however. His empirical proof, the law he formulated, and his political demands were also strongly criticized. That is no wonder; after all, in his analysis he attacked some of the cornerstones of neoliberal ideology: that the market is merely a neutral place in which everyone can in principle pursue and find happiness; that differences in income and wealth are to be welcomed, since they motivate individuals to achieve; and that these differences are legitimate, since they reflect different levels of performance or preferences of market-individuals. At this point, we will name eight such points of criticism that played a central role in the media.

The growth of inequality is not inevitable
Hans-Werner Sinn, head of the Munich-based economic research institute CESifo, doubted Piketty's law of necessarily increasing inequality.[6] His argument is that, even if the formula $r > g$ is true, one cannot therefore conclude

that the gap between rich and poor is constantly increasing, since the rich also consume their income. Sinn was joined by Harvard economist Martin Feldstein, who wrote that the formula would only imply a trend towards increasing wealth if people lived forever. Since this is not the case, wealth in reality is consumed, shared and wasted. The result is supposedly indeterminate, Piketty's formula thus being irrelevant for questions of wealth distribution.[7]

To criticize the critique: first of all, the idea that owners of wealth are not becoming richer because they consume their growth in income contradicts all data – not just that surveyed by Piketty – according to which the concentration of wealth is increasing. Furthermore, it is statistically proven that 'the rich' not only save, but also that their savings rate is higher than that of poorer households.[8] This is also immediately plausible: the more money somebody has, the more readily they can put some aside. Those, on the other hand, who have less money tend to use it up completely for consumption. Albert F. Reiterer finds Sinn's objection to Piketty merely 'amusing'.[9]

The objections that Sinn, Feldstein and others *logically* raise, others see as *empirically* confirmed: an inevitable fundamental tendency towards more inequality is not even proved by Piketty's data, according to the criticism of German economist Peter Bofinger: Piketty's numbers show that, in the period until 1913, the rate of growth of wealth (r) was in fact greater than the growth of national income (g). But Bofinger claims this is not true for the period from 1913 to 2012. Here, claims Bofinger, the rate of return on capital was actually below that of production – and that stands in direct contradiction to Piketty's basic thesis, that r > g.

It should be noted regarding this critique that Bofinger's argument is incorrect, since he considers returns on investment *after* taxes. Pre-tax returns on investment – 'market returns' – are above g in Piketty's work. The fact that, for a while, they were lower after taxes supports Piketty's demands for state intervention and a wealth tax in order to correct market results.[10]

Clive Crook's objection is better.[11] Crook concedes that Piketty proves that r is usually greater than g. 'The trouble is, he also shows that capital-to-output ratios in Britain and France in the 18th and 19th centuries, when r exceeded g by very wide margins, were stable, not rising inexorably.' According to Crook, Piketty says on the one hand that r > g merely tends to lead to an increasing wealth gap. On the other hand, he turns it into an iron law with far-reaching consequences. Crook claims there is a gap between Piketty's rather careful statistical approach on the one hand, in which he constantly points out the uncertainty of the available data and contradictory distributive forces, and on the other hand Piketty's apodictic statements, for example that the long-term consequences of the wealth distribution dynamic is 'frightening'. That is also the basis of criticism by, for example, the US economist Daron Acemoğlu and the Harvard political scientist James Robinson (who became famous for their book *Why Nations Fail: The Origins of Power, Prosperity, and Poverty*): Piketty develops a theory on the basis of history in order 'to understand the past or predict the future' and formulates 'a theory of the long-run tendencies of capitalism' – and like Marx, supposedly overstrains historical research.[12]

We offer the following observation in this regard: Piketty, with his 'law' of growing inequality, indeed merely formulates a tendency, the effects of which, according to Piketty, depend upon different factors and measures. His bleak warnings are not based upon a postulated automatic mechanism, but rather upon a model, under the assumption that the trends of the last thirty years will continue: further weak growth in economic performance and a further decline in the taxation of capital gains and wealth. Whether this will lead to growing inequality is merely probable, not certain: his model merely describes 'only one of several possible future directions for the distribution of wealth. ... It is possible to imagine public institutions and policies that would counter the effects of this implacable logic.'[13] That last sentence shows that the critique by Acemoğlu and Robinson, among others, that Piketty neglects institutions and other societal effects, is not accurate, even if there is room for debate about how seriously Piketty conceptually considers the possibility of counter-developments, the complexity of interrelations, and the influence of other factors, instead of just mentioning them.

Inequality is good

A second thread of critique recognizes growing inequality, but regards it as unproblematic. Thus the British business magazine *The Economist* argues that more inequality does not always lead to political instability. Many democracies have mastered such challenges without an uprising.

Other critics of Piketty see the unequal distribution of income and wealth as a logical and welcome consequence of differences in performance. That is the classical liberal perspective. 'Economic freedom and the enormous innovative power of our economic order, based upon protected private property simply necessitates that there are more successful and less successful participants in the economy.'[14] The unequal distribution of wealth is supposed to be an incentive and reward for outstanding performance, argues the magazine *Wirtschaftswoche*. This incentive mechanism creates prosperity that everyone profits from: 'the (relative) inequality is as great today as in the nineteenth century? Maybe. But what does that say? To put it provocatively, was inequality ever as nice as it is today?'[15]

Since, from this point of view, the strength of capitalism is based upon incentives and rewards, redistribution in favour of more equality leads to less economic growth. 'The political conclusions that Piketty draws from his material would rob the economy and society of their dynamic quality and thus intensify the problem they're supposed to solve.'[16] The fear is that increases in productivity and innovations will fail to materialize: 'When the state confiscates higher incomes, does that really have no consequences for labour productivity? What would've happened if the American tax authorities had taken away the money of Bill Gates, Steve Jobs, or Michael Dell?'[17]

It must be noted that this critique assumes that income and wealth reflect the 'performance' or 'efficiency' of individuals. Leaving aside the question as to whether or not this is accurate (it is not, as we shall see later), Piketty also holds the opinion that this connection exists, or at least that it should. However, this is decreasingly the case with growing inequality. Piketty's argument is based upon the fact – and this will be increasingly the case in the future – that the income of the rich is not based upon performance, but results from inheritance; it is therefore 'unearned' income. That is, it is in fact not performance-focused, but inhibits people's motivation. Thus the neoliberal critique of Piketty also misses its target. Finally, Piketty himself admits: 'Inequality is not necessarily bad in itself: the key question is to decide whether it is justified, whether there are reasons for it.'[18]

Miscalculated

Other critics focus their objections on Piketty's numerical values. First, his calculations were rejected entirely: 'The arguments are adventurous. The mere notion that one could measure the global economy of a thousand or two thousand years ago and calculate the returns on all capital investments back then!' But since this objection is not elaborated, it remains a mere assertion, even if it seems likely.

The British newspaper the *Financial Times* (*FT*) ultimately accused Piketty of miscalculating. He allegedly attributed some numbers to the wrong years, arbitrarily reinterpreted others, and mixed them up. According to the *FT*, if one simplifies and adjusts the data, then there is no evidence of an increase in wealth inequality in Europe since 1970. The sources for the US also '[do not support] the view that the wealth share of the top 1 per cent has increased in the past few decades'.[19]

Piketty replied to these critics that, first, one could not accuse him of intentional falsification, since he had made all of his data and statistics freely available on the internet – open to improvements and critique. Secondly, he acknowledged that the available data were not optimal. More recent calculations, however, still supported his theses.[20] Even after the proposed corrections by the *FT*, nothing is changed with regard to the fundamental tendency of income distribution.

Many economists agreed with this stance. Even if the *FT* had been correct, the consequences for Piketty's thesis would have been minimal, decided *Forbes Magazine*.[21] In the *Guardian*, Howard Reed accused the *FT* of not taking into consideration a change of methodology in the case of Britain. 'To believe that the Giles series represents an accurate picture of the evolution of wealth inequality in the UK over the last 50 years, one would have to believe that the wealth share of the top 10% really did fall by 12 percentage points during the 1970s, and by another 11 percentage points between 2005 and 2006. Does anyone really believe this? Of course not.'[22] For the business journalist Ulrike Herrmann, it is therefore 'somewhat odd' that the *Financial Times* 'in an article that was widely read internationally, attacked the data, of all things, as "flawed"'.[23] According to Herrmann, Piketty uses the standard method of combining tax statistics and household surveys. 'It was therefore easy for him to refute the *Financial Times* and make them look ridiculous.' Other economists, especially from the US, also pointed out that all available statistics proved a growth of wealth in particular for the super-rich. The *FT*'s critique fizzled out.

Piketty and his colleagues admit that the preparation of the data is rather problematic. They say it is difficult to clarify what exactly counts as wealth (and what does not) over large timespans and in comparison between multiple countries. The researchers also bring up tax fraud and tax evasion, which might falsify the data. 'The rich, in particular, have a strong incentive to understate their taxable incomes.' Piketty's doctoral candidate Gabriel Zucman has specialized in tax evasion and havens.[24] Those responsible for maintaining the databank also name further limits to the numerical data: inequalities otherwise independent of income are not taken into consideration; the numbers for all incomes are 'before taxes', that is, they do not take state redistribution into consideration; in some countries, sometimes individual incomes are counted, sometimes household incomes, which makes a comparison difficult.

No problem in Germany

A specifically German strain of the critique of Piketty points out that although inequality is an important topic for the United States, it is not for Germany: 'The Frenchman has written the right book at the right time for America.' In this context, the Cologne Institute for Economic Research – financed by business – noted that in recent times, the gap between rich and poor has not further widened in Germany. 'Since 2005, income inequality has remained about constant.'[25]

Regarding this critique, it must be noted that in his book Piketty finds tendencies at work in Germany similar to those of other industrialized countries. The fact that inequality has not increased in Germany since 2005 is due to the short timespan under observation, not an argument against Piketty. Furthermore, the Cologne Institute for Economic Research considers only the development of income and not that of wealth. And, in the case of the latter, the situation is unambiguous: in no other eurozone country is wealth so unequally distributed as in Germany. The richest 1 per cent of households in Germany own about one-third of total wealth, the richest 5 per cent own about 50 per cent. For the US, the corresponding numbers are 35 and 60, respectively.[26]

So much for the economically liberal critiques of Piketty's book. But leftist economists also had critiques of their own.

Piketty's work is situated within the neoclassical mainstream!

Economic science is characterized by different 'schools', which do not only differ in terms of their fundamental theoretical assumptions, but also fundamentally contradict one another. It is therefore no wonder that economists with an orientation towards John Maynard Keynes and Karl Marx raised criticisms: they pointed out that Piketty's empirical research was important, but that he shared premises with the economic mainstream, the neoclassical school. Thus Jakob Kapeller from the Institute of Philosophy and Economic Theory at the University of Linz criticized Piketty's 'eagerness not to dupe specific professional circles and their cherished theories too strongly'. That has problematic consequences: 'In practice, this seems to require that all empirical findings must be somehow aligned with the established mode of mainstream theorizing. This dangerous concoction of critical data-driven research and an overemphasis on theoretical modesty and respect tends to run into contradictions.' Piketty does not address these contradictions. Rather, 'the implied neoclassical coherence of the argument brings about the unfortunate circumstance that potentially enriching arguments from sociological or heterodox research generally remain disregarded', despite Piketty's wholehearted professions to the contrary in the introduction.[27]

The American economist James K. Galbraith and the leftist publicist Benjamin Kunkel, who helped to found the cultural journal *n+1*, make similar arguments.[28] Both criticize Piketty for not seriously taking into consideration the critique of the neoclassical mainstream formulated by the economist Piero Sraffa (editor of the works of David Ricardo, contemporary of Keynes and a friend of Antonio Gramsci) and the work following in his wake. Briefly addressing this critique,[29] Piketty even incorrectly summarizes the positions of those involved. What was the subject of debate back then? In the 1950s and 1960s, it had been demonstrated that neoclassical economics was built on sand: in its construction of models, it assumed a one-good economy – that is, an economy that consists of a single, homogeneous good, for example wheat: a construction completely divorced from reality. However, if this premise is abandoned, neoclassical economics cannot make any resilient macroeconomic statements, for example concerning the connection between the level of wages and unemployment or technological rationalization. Piketty ignores this critique, for example in the case of his statements and propositions he raises regarding the role of technological progress in economic development. Ulrike Herrmann pointedly states: 'So we can just write off Piketty as a theorist.'

The Marxist geographer David Harvey, on the other hand, criticizes the fact that Piketty does not provide a reason for the development towards more inequality. Even regularities in the data sets do not amount to theory, and he polemicizes: 'the law is the law and that is that.' Piketty's theoretical gap, according to Harvey, is rooted in the fact that, in line with neoclassical theory, he understands capital as a thing and not as a process, as a social relation.[30] Rainer Rilling makes a virtue of the necessity that Piketty is not able to escape the neoclassical mainstream and advances the argument that Piketty's empirical results are interesting precisely 'because they come from the mainstream and possibly indicate or allow for further-reaching shifts in its ideological field'.[31]

Blind spots: politics and social struggles

In Piketty's bird's-eye view of the last 200 years, depth of focus is lost in terms of how questions of social distribution are actually negotiated – in social struggles. That is how the critique of Doug Henwood, David Graeber and others can be understood. 'The major frustration of the book is political', writes Henwood, publisher of the American newsletter *Left Business Observer* and author of *Wall Street: How It Works and for Whom.*[32] Piketty does not deal with the question of which political forces affect inequality and the wage ratio. Piketty ignores 'the most obvious' reason for the lower capital–income ratio, according to Graeber.[33] After 1945, the capitalist system 'faced a global rival in the Soviet bloc, revolutionary anti-capitalist movements from Uruguay to China, and at least the possibility of workers' uprisings at home'. High rates of growth back then were not simply followed by redistribution. Rather, 'capitalists felt the need to buy off at least some portion of the working classes, placed more money in ordinary people's hands, creating increasing consumer demand that was itself largely responsible for the remarkable rates of economic growth that marked capitalism's "golden age".' In the meantime, however, every serious political threat has disappeared, and capitalism has gone back to its 'normal state: that is, to savage inequalities'. The change, Joachim Bischoff and Bernhard Müller would agree here,[34] cannot be explained without the structural transformation, the decline of the trade unions as well as a change in business leadership and culture. Hagen Krämer points out that this act of ignoring social struggles is not a coincidence, but rather the necessary result of neoclassical theory: 'within the framework of such a model, income distribution, as Piketty himself writes in some passages, is determined exclusively "technically". There is no room for a consideration of the influence of power upon distribution.'[35]

The financial markets are part of the problem
Despite his important insights, Piketty was criticized for not recognizing the importance of financial markets for the developments he posits. Thus, Fabian Lindner of the Macroeconomic Policy Institute, closely associated with German trade unions, writes that up through the nineteenth century, wealth had physical limits (land, industrial facilities). It was first with the increasing importance of financial markets and the paper assets traded on them that the growth of capital no longer had a material limit. Bischoff and Müller make a similar argument, albeit with a different emphasis: Piketty does not consider 'the dynamic of a growing supply of money capital' which has had as a consequence a decline in interest rates since the 1980s and which has led to 'a rise in the price of securities and real estate'.[36] Thus the thesis r > g is insufficiently argued. The declining power of wage labourers also cannot be explained without *The Rule of Financial Markets*, the title of a book by Joachim Bischoff. Precisely because Piketty criticizes 'income without work' from wealth, a critique of the dominance of financial markets must be part of the argument, according to Bischoff and Müller.

Eurocentrism
Chandran Nair, director of the Global Institute for Tomorrow (Gift) based in Hong Kong, criticizes[37] the fact that Piketty's analysis disregards the inequality produced in the third world by Western colonialism. Piketty 'ignores the context in which western wealth creation occurred, despite the fact that many seek to perpetuate and emulate it today'. His book is furthermore Eurocentric: a comparison between the United States and India or China would make it clear that the focus upon the 'Western world' is an unacceptable blind spot. Not only does a large share of the world population live in both countries; an extreme inequality also reigns in them, despite

the fact that in global rankings of billionaires, India occupies sixth place.

Furthermore, says Nair, Piketty does not consider natural resources, due to his theoretical approach; ultimately, millions of people 'are not even part of the economic system', and 'helping them is not a matter of increasing economic capital but rather protecting and equitably distributing natural capital'.

It should be noted that contrary to Nair's critique, Piketty does not disregard colonialism, but he does raise it from the perspective of the colonial powers. In this sense, Nair's critique is justified. But Nair himself suppresses evidence that, for example, China in the meantime has become a colonial power in parts of Africa, which is why Piketty mentions China's rise as an economic power.[38] Against this background, it is again consistent that Piketty deals with China rather than India, although the data situation for India must be somewhat better, as the World Top Incomes Database shows.[39]

It is a completely different question when one considers how Nair seeks to defend 'natural capital' against 'economic capital'. In light of the global destruction of nature and climate change, this concern is right and important, but it cannot be asserted by characterizing material wealth (nature) as 'capital'. Rather, nature must be protected against the capitalist logic of validation. In this sense, an ecological perspective cannot be held without a critique of capitalism.

In general, the critiques of Piketty's book – despite the last few mentioned exceptions – have remained trapped within the framework of the neoclassical mainstream. The statistical material was hardly criticized – with the exception of the *Financial Times* – and when it was, then only tentatively and without consequences. The tendency was that Piketty's central thesis – the concentration of income and wealth – was substantially shared and his statistical calculation effort praised. Part of the critique formulated of Piketty's statements cannot therefore be regarded as a counterposition to the Piketty hype, but rather as part of the hype.

CHAPTER 5

Capital in the Twenty-First Century – What to Make of It?

In this final chapter, we will critically evaluate the book. What has Piketty achieved – and what has he not? How accurate is his critique of conditions – and what standard ideologies are transmitted by *Capital in the Twenty-First Century*? Here we will deal less with his economic demands, but rather with critical social questions that he poses or does not pose.

Piketty's merits

Even critics concede that Piketty has initiated an important discussion with his book: 'it doesn't matter if Piketty is wrong', writes Mark Whitehouse.[1] 'The argument itself reflects a desirable shift in the field of economics toward answering questions that really matter.' Reiterer puts it more drastically: the hype around Piketty 'shows that a certain discontent reigns even among capital's watchdogs'.[2] 'The bourgeoisie has afforded itself a moment of self-reflection' according to Felix Klopotek in the leftist monthly magazine *Konkret*. Critique of, as well as agreement with, Piketty's work thus reflects a real problem, a quandary that the social elite is embroiled in. What does the problem consist of? The condition of the economy and state finances of most industrialized countries: on the one hand, the growth of total economic performance is relatively weak, in the US as well as in Europe and Japan. This trend could persist, according to the OECD. Between 2010 and 2020, global growth will amount to 3.6 per cent annually, but in the years up to 2060 – if trends remain constant – it will sink to 2.4 per cent annually.

Social inequality, according to the OECD, will therefore increase.[3]

Due to weak economic growth, it will become increasingly difficult to 'grow out of' the debts accumulated in the last few years; that is to say, it will be increasingly difficult to contrast increasing debts with a corresponding growth in economic performance from which the debts can be serviced. The credit worthiness of states – that is, the trust of financiers in the financial solidity of governments – is thus also permanently endangered. Among other things, the growth of financial wealth increases along with the debts of states – as well as those of businesses and households. This wealth – as credit, bonds and other securities – represents claims. They are thus claims worth billions upon yields that must be produced in the future. If these claims are not redeemed, a further financial crash threatens. In this manner, the bourgeoisie is taking note that there is an overaccumulation, and overproduction of capital; that is, too much capital measured in terms of profitable possibilities for investment.

States are partially attempting to tax this wealth. Thus, there is supposed to be a tax on financial transactions in Europe; tax havens are to be 'drained'; the EU and the US are attempting to make it more difficult for businesses to shift their tax burden via transnational corporate structures to those countries where taxes are lower; banks in Europe are to be obligated to pay billions into resolution funds that will spring into action in the case of bankruptcies. In Germany, for example, further ideas are being discussed, such as the introduction of a wealth tax or duty, the replacement of the settlement tax by a progressive taxation of capital gains according to income tax, the reform of the inheritance tax, and raising the property tax. In 2014 in France, where Piketty advises the Socialist Party, a supertax on the rich of 75 per cent was introduced.

On the one hand, there is thus a certain financial need

on the part of states. On the other hand, attempts at taxing capital always run up against the same limit: the competition between states for investors. No state wants to scare away investors with taxes that are too high. The consequence is a competition for low taxes between countries for the 'skittish' capital.[4] Thus the OECD also emphasizes that the taxation of 'mobile' factors such as capital will be increasingly difficult in the future. According to the OECD, increasing international cooperation between states – that is, an end to or ameliora- tion of tax competition between them – is necessary in order to prevent the erosion of the tax base of the state.

This is Piketty's starting point, and he advocates a wealth tax that is to be internationally coordinated and implemented. Even if this proposal – due to the contradiction just set out – has an 'illusory character', Piketty has at least ignited a broad debate about the taxation of wealth and inequality and redis- tribution. That is the merit of his book. Furthermore, his statistical data concerning inequality and the concentration of wealth offers material that critics of the reigning economic system can use – the question is *how*, which leads us to the critique.

Mistakes, gaps, ideological legends

Piketty supports his insights, as we have seen, with com- prehensive statistical material. He presents himself less as a theoretician than as a sort of neutral statistician who allows the numbers to speak for themselves. Among other things, his intuitive formula $r > g$ is nothing other than a statistical indi- cator. But numbers never speak for themselves; they have to be interpreted. And that also happens in Piketty's book. At its foundation is a certain interpretation of the entire economic process: that of the so-called neoclassical school, which dom- inates universities and textbooks, according to which the free forces of the market lead to equilibrium. According to the economic mainstream, this constitutes a social optimum, a condition of the greatest possible satisfaction of needs. The fact that the statistical material he has prepared contradicts this is indeed clear to Piketty, but he draws no theoretical consequences from this. Thus Piketty is not only not comparable to Marx, as he himself tirelessly emphasizes, but also not even with Keynes, who at least consummated a break with the theoretical foundations of the neoclassical mainstream.

Capitalism

Piketty regards the dominant economic system completely positively. All of his criticisms of conditions and their development are not intended as a principled objection to the capitalist mode of production and distribution. The ideal condition he strives for is a prosperous capitalism characterized by economic growth. Critique of growth as such is foreign to Piketty. And he only criticizes inequality to the extent that it could damage growth and the legitimacy of capitalism. In this sense, he is both progressive and conservative: he wants to change something in order to maintain social relations as they are. He wants to protect capitalism from the poor – not the other way around. That's not anything that one has to 'uncover', but rather it is his openly formulated 'programme': 'I admire capitalism; I admire private property, and I admire the market economy. Of course I recognize that economic growth occurs principally in capitalism. Of course I cling to private property, because it is the foundation of our freedom. There was never as much capital as today. I was 18 years old, when the Berlin Wall fell. I belong to a generation that never had sympathy for Communism.'[5]

Despite all admiration for capitalism, however, Piketty shows no interest for the particularities of this economic form, and doesn't ask himself what capitalism is. He also has no concept of capital, since he equates wealth and capital. A piece of land, a building, a sum of money or a production facility are for him simply 'possessions' or 'property'.

The economic form in which this property exists and the manner in which it organizes social reproduction does not interest him. His formula r > g is supposed to be eternally valid, in feudalism as well as capitalism. However, it is precisely this narrow-mindedness, this heedlessness with regard to the specific social character of wealth that leads him to trace the historical development of inequality, but only on the basis of already presupposed inequality, which for him 'simply exists'. Because Piketty flirts with Marx but does not consider him seriously, he loses sight of things, especially the essential aspect of that which he seeks to explain.

Wealth is a form of property. Property, however, is not a universal principle according to which somebody has power of disposition over a thing (in pre-capitalist societies, namely, that was not the case in such a generalized sense). Rather, at a very general level, the property relation encompasses the appropriation of nature by human beings. This metabolic process (*Stoffwechsel*) is consummated with the aid of three elements: nature is the raw material, the instruments for processing nature are the instruments of labour, and the results of this processing of labour are the fruits, the means for reproducing human life. These three elements are the objective conditions of production. A further condition is that each individual belongs to a community (*Gemeinwesen*). Access to nature, appropriation, cannot be executed by a human being who is isolated and grows up alone. And the mode in which the individual relates to these conditions historically characterizes the various modes of property relations. The differences between pre-capitalist and capitalist forms of production can only be established in terms of *how* individuals relate to the means of production and the fruits of their labour. This in turn depends upon *how* the relation of individuals to the community is regulated; that is, which social form these relations assume. To take the example of the European Middle Ages: ownership of the means of production and the fruits of labour without ownership of land characterized the existence of artisans as members of a guild; serfs, on the other hand, had disposal over their own means of production and the land, but had to yield part of the fruits of their labour in the form of goods in kind to their lords (or perform corvée).[6]

With his theoretical conception, Marx is not only able to distinguish between capitalist and pre-capitalist modes of production; he can also identify comprehensible differences within the latter category. For Piketty, in contrast, all cats are grey, since they all somehow labour and they all somehow have wealth – and always have. Piketty generalizes bourgeois forms in an ahistorical manner; in past forms of wealth and inequality, he merely recognizes the bourgeois forms, projects them into the past, and thus presents them as eternally valid – bourgeois relations appear as both transhistorical and natural at the same time. Piketty, however, is not alone with this 'procedure'. Rather, it is characteristic of bourgeois theory that it only rarely elucidates its own historical character, concentrated instead on the historical character of other societies that are historically or 'culturally' part of the past or far away.

So what is particular about capitalist forms of property? For one thing, the separation of producers from the means of production, which can be referred to as 'inequality of the first order', whereby according to Marx 'the positing of the individual as a *worker*, who is stripped of all qualities except this one, is itself a *historical* product'.[7] Labour-power first became a commodity when human beings were excluded from the possibility of providing for themselves through agriculture; they were formally free and equal, to the extent that personal relations of ownership and dependency were no longer dominant.

For another thing, capitalism is characterized by the conditions under which that which is separated (labour-power and means of production) is once again united: both –

labour-power and means of production – are reunited as capital, that is to say as a social relation that valorizes, increases, a previously advanced sum of value.[8] The aim of valorization is the essential characteristic distinguishing capitalist property relations from pre-capitalist epochs in which production occurred with a 'use-value orientation'; that is, not blindly driven by a dynamic of making more capital from capital. The same holds for the forces of production, the development of which was not a technical but rather a social question. Marx reports in *Capital* on prohibitions and even more drastic methods to prevent an increase in the productivity of labour.[9] The siphoning off of surplus product also did not follow capitalist logic: the ruling classes in pre-capitalist societies engaged in exploitation for wants and needs that were historically specific: for a representative life, for the favour of God by endowing the construction of large religious buildings, and in order to wage wars. The aim of exploitation was not the accumulation of capital as an end in itself. Piketty loses sight of all these differences.

Inequality, like wealth, is all the same to Piketty as well, and he thus moves within a partially illuminated, bourgeois horizon. Before capitalism, and here Piketty would still agree, inequality appeared to be God-given, corresponding to a 'natural' social order – not even people were equal. In an 'enlightened' society, in contrast, such a pattern of legitimation is tough to swallow. Others have taken its place, however, which among other things are cultivated by the great thinkers of bourgeois theory – including Piketty. For example, the notion that labour justifies property and therefore wealth – that is regarded as the norm. John Locke (1632–1704) was the first to trace property back to labour: 'Whatsoever then he removes out of the state that nature hath provided, and left it in, he hath mixed his labour with, and joined to it something that is his own, and thereby makes it his property.'[10] This proposition is not only found up to today in economic theory, but is deeply rooted in everyday common sense – albeit not without contradictions. On the one hand, inequality appears to be only explainable in terms of different levels of labour performance and therefore only legitimate in terms of labour performance; on the other hand, reality shows that this is not the case. That is the background as to why Piketty moves in circles. He thus ends up arguing that inequality is growing because inequality exists. He argues in a circular fashion, without explaining how 'original' inequality came into the world at all, and which socially specific inequality characterizes capitalism: the separation of direct producers from the objective possibilities of production. Piketty thus has noticeably little to say about the manner in which inequality arises and persists in capitalism. That has consequences.

Performance

The quintessence of Piketty's analysis of inequality and its development is: with the increasing division of society, inheritances become increasingly important, and this is becoming a problem. Why? 'Our democratic societies rest on a meritocratic worldview, or at any rate a meritocratic hope, by which I mean a belief in a society in which equality is based more on merit and effort than on kinship and rents.'[11]

It remains unclear whether Piketty shares this belief and worldview and whether he regards such a 'meritocratic' capitalism – that is to say, one based upon the principle of performance – as at all realizable, or merely as an unfulfillable hope for which one should at least strive. But what should such a meritocracy look like? In such a world, everyone would receive their 'fair' share of wealth according to their 'performance'. The performance of 'workers' consists in their labour performance. The performance of capitalists consists for one thing in the fact that they risk part of their wealth – ultimately every investment is laden with risk. For another thing, the return or interest that capitalists receive is a reward for forgoing consumption – after all, the capitalist could have also made a nice life for himself with the money. That is the dominant narrative, which contains multiple errors.

Concerning risk: it is true that whoever lends money takes the risk that he or she might not see that money ever again. And the greater this risk is, the greater the interest demanded will tend to be. That does not mean, however, that interest is the 'just wage' for risk. In fact, the reverse is the case: capitalists want to increase their money, make a return on it. That is their goal. To do that, however, they have to take a risk. Their profit is not compensation for a risk. On the contrary: the risk is the condition for the profit. The profit motive comes first. A car company also does not want to produce and distribute cars, thus taking on a risk and receiving profits as 'compensation' for the risk. The risk is, by the way, not something natural, but rather socially conditioned: in capitalism, an investment is risky because all competitors want to make profits and struggle with each other for market share, but not all are able to succeed. To state things more generally: in a society in which production is not regulated in a cooperative and political manner, but rather commodities are produced for an anonymous market, it is only revealed in retrospect whether the investment was worth it, whether the product produced is actually sold. The entrepreneurial risk thus arises not solely through the profit orientation, but already due to production for an anonymous market.

Concerning abstention from consumption: interest or returns are not compensation for the investor investing the money rather than going shopping with it. Interest as 'compensation for abstaining from consumption': behind that is always the notion that the wealthy would prefer to buy yachts, palaces, caviar and sports cars, but abstain from that in favour of investing. That is a reckless notion. As if the total invested financial wealth worldwide amounting to about 200 trillion US dollars is actually intended for a shopping spree. As if, for example, the capital invested in Volkswagen is actually the shopping budget of a capitalist household. The assumption that 'profit = compensation for abstaining from consumption' is based upon the idea that money is merely a means of purchase and negates the immediate purpose that money has as capital – and after all, we live in capitalism: it should constantly increase, accumulate. Capital is in fact not a thing, but a permanent movement.

Concerning the wage: people's income is supposed to correspond to their performance. For workers, this results in the belief in a 'fair day's wage for a fair day's work'. This extraordinarily beloved idea ranks among the central legitimizing ideologies of capitalism. It is the basis of the notion that the wage is paid for performance, that is to say for labour, and that the worker is thus justly compensated, or is supposed to be. That this is not the case can already be recognized in how 'performance' is measured. Of what does the 'performance' of workers consist? In the number of pieces produced per hour? Hardly. If the goods produced are not sold, the performance is equal to zero, regardless of how much work was done. 'Strictly speaking, there is no fixed performance, because what a concrete effort is worth economically depends upon whether there is a demand for the product on the market, and what price is paid for it. If paying demand grows, the effort is worth more.'[12] If people work and their product does not sell, then 'without a doubt they've made an effort, but considered economically have not performed'. Performance or productivity depends accordingly upon the market success of a company – whether the company makes a profit. 'Productivity is ultimately not a measure for the diligence and effort of the employees, but rather of the success of the company.'[13]

What Gert G. Wagner, an economist at the German Institute for Economic Research, is describing here is analyzed by Marx in his major work *Capital* (which, according to Piketty, is too complicated: 'I never managed really to read it. I mean I don't know if you've tried to read it. Have you tried?'[14]). The wage does not pay for labour, but rather for the disposal of labour-power for a specific period of time. During working time, the enterprise applies labour in order to make a profit – that is to say, to extract output from the workers that has a monetary value greater than that which they receive as a wage. That is possible because only the disposal over the ability to perform labour (labour-power) is paid, and the workers do not receive a wage corresponding to the value product produced by their labour. That is how it is possible in the first place that the success of the business can be measured in terms of profits – in terms of that which the workers precisely do *not* receive: surplus-labour. The struggle for shares of social income occurs permanently, its foundation is a negative dependence: capital and labour need each other, but at the same time stand in opposition to each other.

Harmony
Wealth in capitalism arises because wage-labourers produce more than they receive, and capital is thus valorized. The wage level is not measured in terms of individual labour effort or the concrete product of labour, but rather in terms of power relations on the labour market. When unemployment is high, those seeking jobs compete with each other for a few positions. This allows businesses to depress wages, and the reverse is true: when labour-power is scarce, trade unions can impose higher wages. The fact that the wage is based upon power relations on the labour market is the entire reason why workers organized themselves in trade unions: in order to minimize their individual susceptibility to extortion.

Nonetheless, in negotiations over wages, wage workers tend to be the weaker party, since they have no wealth or other possibilities to secure their existence other than the sale of their labour-power. In Piketty's work, this 'state of affairs', this social relation, this 'inequality of the first order', is simply presupposed: capitalists 'just have' capital, the wage-labouring population 'is just' without property. For Piketty – as for the entire mainstream of economic theory – that is a quasi-natural condition. As outlined above, this separation of those without means on one side and the wealthy on the other is not natural, but rather had first to be historically imposed.

The distribution of the 'factors of production' capital and labour, however, is not an object of study for neoclassical theory – nor for Piketty. For Piketty, there are no classes any more, no antagonism between capital and labour. For him, society consists merely of individuals with more or less 'wealth'. There is only a *quantitative* difference, because workers also have wealth and capitalists also work – just differing by degree. What gets lost in the shuffle is that the owner-occupied home of a wage-labourer is a completely different *qualitative* form of wealth than the car factory of a capitalist. According to Piketty, however, both contribute their share to the whole, to increasing 'economic performance'. Gross domestic product appears as a communal effort. All antagonisms are thus erased.

Justice
There is never a 'meritocracy' – a 'just' correspondence between performance and income – in capitalism. However, the idea of a just income is useful: it justifies conditions in which a discussion about just wages occurs, but not one about the relations of disposition and power that actually underlie and regulate income. This legitimizing function is what Piketty has in mind when he warns against growing inequality. What does he see as the central problem of growing inequality and the concentration of wealth? The fact that wealth is increasingly distributed through inheritances and not through performance. With that – and only with that – inequality becomes injustice and thus a problem for Piketty,

since inheritance is a way of transmitting wealth that is not mediated by the market, which he regards as scandalous. His demand is that only the market should decide the distribution of income. The market is for him the central entity of justice: market results are fair results.

Piketty, as already mentioned, leaves the reader in the dark about whether he himself regards such a meritocracy as possible. However, he certainly wishes to rescue belief in it:

> This belief and this hope play a very crucial role in modern society, for a simple reason: in a democracy, the professed equality of rights of all citizens contrasts sharply with the very real inequality of living conditions, and in order to overcome this contradiction it is vital to make sure that social inequalities derive from rational and universal principles rather than arbitrary contingencies. Inequalities must therefore be just and useful to all, at least in the realm of discourse and as far as possible in reality as well.[15]

> It also bears emphasizing that the role of meritocratic beliefs in justifying inequality in modern societies is evident not only at the top of hierarchy but lower down as well, as an explanation for the disparity between the lower and middle classes.[16]

With a wealth tax, Piketty seeks to rescue liberal ideology – everyone is the master of his or her own fate – from the results of the market. He wants to restore people's belief in a just capitalism, or at least the hope that proverbially dies last. Piketty's warning against inequality can be reduced to a single objection: if the belief in a society that justly rewards performance with legitimate differences in income disappears, then people will start to doubt whether everything is as it should be in capitalism and whether differences between poor and rich are ultimately just. Piketty argues like a crafty technician of power who exhibits concern about the subservience and motivation of the propertyless masses. That distinguishes him significantly from other theorists who work on the topic of inequality who exhibit a certain anger about the social consequences of unequal relations. For example, Göran Therborn: 'Inequality always means excluding some people from something. When it doesn't literally kill people or stunt their lives, inequality means exclusion: excluding people from possibilities produced by human development ... The empirical evidence is undisputable. Inequality kills.'[17]

One finds no such outrage in Piketty's work. Rather, these developments are the point of departure for his concerns about society's powers of integration. Piketty's book and data can therefore only be 'misused' for their own purposes. Piketty is politically and theoretically conservative, even if he devotes himself to the topic of inequality.

Success
The performance ideology that Piketty promotes moves – particularly in Germany – within a dangerous context. Performance ideology goes hand in hand with a chauvinism of affluence, which is expressed in Europe through racism and a hatred for supposedly 'unproductive' people, for example 'lazy Greeks'.[18]

The idea of a performance-linked income also has a flipside: if the market is recognized as an entity for evaluating performance, then economic failure can consistently be explained by a lack of potential and willingness to perform. Greece is in crisis? Then the Greeks surely have not worked hard enough. Somebody is unemployed? Then he or she obviously did not make enough of an effort. Somebody earns very little? Then he or she is not worth more. Somebody earns a lot of money? Then he or she is an excellent character who possesses saleable 'skills': the ability to perform, assertiveness, the capacity for teamwork, in short: the ability to succeed. Every result of the market can thus be explained by quasi-natural, personal qualities of individuals, and is therefore justified. Success and failure thus become a question of character.[19]

With that, every critique of the economic system is rendered toothless. Those who succeed can be proud of themselves and look down upon those who fail. Those who fail can admire the winners of the competition and be ashamed – which is to say, turn the critique towards themselves.

This is a development that the middle classes go along with. The sociologist Theodor W. Adorno once described the 'authoritarian character' as one who wishes to maintain its own social position by bowing to those above and kicking those below. That is a dangerous development that cannot be met by fulminating on behalf of a performance focus and against 'unearned' income – regardless of how 'left' this critique sometimes sounds. On the contrary: the central values of bourgeois society such as competition, performance and aspiration must be subject to critique.

What effects change

One of the biggest advocates on behalf of Piketty is the American Nobel Prize winner Paul Krugman, who is responsible for a large part of the Piketty hype. To be sure, Piketty argues in such a neoclassical manner that Krugman, a so-called neo-Keynesian, is also forced to criticize him. Nonetheless, Krugman is full of praise for Piketty's book, since he hopes that the striking development of inequality it documents must provoke a will to change things – towards more redistribution, 'less market', and 'more state'. Piketty is thus supposed to have the same effect as John Maynard Keynes, whose writings after the Second World War considerably changed and put their stamp upon economic policy in Western industrial states. At least that is the usual narrative – which, however, is not true. Keynes's main work, *The General Theory of Employment, Interest and Money* was first published years after the first New Deal measures had been implemented in the United States. So Keynes merely retroactively 'legitimized' what was already being practised politically.

Until 1932, US President Franklin D. Roosevelt had still rejected every debt-financed state intervention. But which argument convinced the politicians? Not Keynes's arguments, but rather the class struggles that were raging in the US and politicized many people: alongside a radical, large self-organized movement of the unemployed, millions of wage-labourers went on strike (particularly in the auto industry) despite the threat of unemployment. In the factories an effective means were the famous sit-down strikes. The labour struggles led to further social struggles and made the trade unions strong, and the number of members multiplied. Capital was forced to recognize the unions as a negotiating partner for collective bargaining, and Congress saw itself compelled to implement a minimum wage and the 40-hour week.[20]

If the compulsory measures of social struggles are not present in a crisis, then concessions cannot be wrung from the state, and politics remains the politics of capital – and modest goals like a tax on wealth remain an illusion. For leftists, there only remains the hope that their arguments are heard, even if they are made by liberal economists like Piketty. That is indeed one of the reasons why there is much attention for such books even among leftists. Whether or not things will move in the right direction, however, is not something decided by bestsellers and op-ed debates, but by social struggles.

Notes

1. Pikettymania

1   See Clea Caulcutt, 'France is Not Impressed with Thomas Piketty', *Foreign Policy*, April 29, 2014 and Tyler Cowen and Veronique de Rugy, 'Why Piketty's Book Is a Bigger Deal in America Than in France', *New York Times*, April 29, 2014.

2. The Prelude: Redistribution, Inequality and Debt Crisis

1   Interview with Hans-Werner Sinn, WSM-Nachrichten, June 2005.

2   Steffen Ganghof and Philipp Genschel, 'Taxation and Democracy in the EU', *Journal of European Public Policy*, 15:1, January 2008, p. 64.

3   Eurostat, *Taxation Trends in the European Union, Data for the EU Member States and Norway*, European Communities, 2009, p. 105.

4   Ganghof and Genschel, p. 64.

5   Engelbert Stockhammer, *Why Have Wage Shares Fallen? A Panel Analysis of the Determinants of Functional Income Distribution*, Conditions of Work and Employment Series No. 35, International Labour Office, 2013.

6   Organisation for Economic Co-operation and Development, *Growing Unequal?: Income Distribution and Poverty in OECD Countries*, OECD, Organisation for Economic Co-operation and Development, Paris, 2008 and Organisation for Economic Co-operation and Development, *Divided We Stand*, OECD, Organisation for Economic Co-operation and Development, Paris, 2011.

7   Ibid.

8   See Birgit Mahnkopf, *Formel 1 der neuen Sozialdemokratie: Gerechtigkeit durch Ungleichheit. Zur Neuinterpretation der sozialen Frage im globalen Kapitalismus*, Prokla 121, 2000, p. 489–525.

9   The European Central Bank even admitted this with regard to 'the case of Greece' in 2009 (Working paper: *The Janus-Headed*

Salvation), but for obvious reasons this was not shouted from the rooftops.

10 Organisation for Economic Co-operation and Development, *All on Board. Making Inclusive Growth Happen*, OECD, Organisation for Economic Co-operation and Development, Paris, 2014.

11 Natixis, *Very High Debt Ratios: Why Is This a Problem?*, Flash Economics, 2014.

12 A well-known 'self-critique' was provided by Paul Krugman, 'How Did Economists Get It So Wrong?', *New York Times Magazine*, September 2, 2009.

13 An overview of the diverse and rather contradictory attempts at explanation is provided by Trevor Evans, *Verlauf und Erklärungsfaktoren der herrschenden ökonomischen Lehre. Der ökonomiekritische Diskurs des Cambridge-Ökonomen Piero Sraffa*, Prokla 164, 2011, pp. 347–68.

14 Michael Kumhof and Romain Ranciere, *Inequality, Leverage and Crises*, IMF Working Paper 10/268, International Monetary Fund, 2010.

15 Michael Kumhof, Romain Ranciere, and Pablo Winant, *Inequality, Leverage and Crises: The Case of Endogenous Default*, IMF Working Paper 13/249, International Monetary Fund, 2013.

16 Stephan Kaufmann, 'Der neue Sinn für Gerechtigkeit', *Frankfurter Rundschau*, May 16, 2014.

17 Andrew G. Berg and Jonathan D. Ostry, *Inequality and Unsustainable Growth: Two Sides of the Same Coin?*, IMF Staff Discussion Note 11/08, International Monetary Fund, 2011.

18 Jonathan D. Ostry, Andrew Berg, and Charlambos G. Tsangarides, *Redistribution, Inequality and Growth*, IMF Staff Discussion Note 14/02, International Monetary Fund, 2014.

19 International Monetary Fund, *Taxing Times: Fiscal Monitor*, October 2013.

20 Charles Moore, 'I'm Starting to Think that the Left Might Actually Be Right', *Daily Telegraph*, July 22, 2011.

21 Frank Schirrmacher, 'Ich beginner zu glauben, dass die Linke recht hat', *Frankfurter Allgemeine Zeitung*, August 15, 2011.

22 Warren E. Buffett, 'Stop Coddling the Super-Rich', *New York Times*, August 14, 2011.

23 From the more-or-less well-known 'greats' such as Göran Therborn, Hans-Ulrich Wehler, Ulrike Herrmann, Ulrich Beck, Michael Hartmann, Jens Beckert, and Zygmunt Bauman.

24   *Apostolic Exhortation Evangelii Gaudium of the Holy Father Francis to the Bishops, Clergy, Consecrated Persons, and the Lay Faithful On the Proclamation of the Gospel in Today's World*, November 24, 2013.

25   Organisation for Economic Co-operation and Development, 'Urgent Action Needed to Tackle Rising Inequality and Social Divisions, Says OECD', Press Release, March 18, 2014.

26   Launch of 'In it Together – Why Less Inequality Benefits All', Remarks by Angel Gurría, Secretary-General, Organisation for Economic Co-operation and Development, Paris, May 21, 2015.

27   Bertelsmann Stiftung, *Bertelsmann Stiftung intensiviert Arbeit an Reformkonzepten für ausgewogene Balance zwischen Wirtschaftswachstum und Chancen auf Teilhabe*, April 29, 2014.

28   Boris Groendahl, 'Central Banks Channel Piketty Inequality Concerns, Nowotny Says', *Bloomberg*, June 7, 2014.

29   Standard & Poor's Ratings Services, *How Increasing Income Inequality Is Dampening U.S. Economic Growth, and Possible Ways to Change the Tide*, McGraw Hill Financial, August 5, 2014; Federico Cingano, *Trends in Income Inequality and Its Impact on Economic Growth*, OECD Social, Employment and Migration Working Papers No. 163, OECD Publishing, Paris, 2014.

3. The Book

1   Thomas Piketty, Harvard University Press, 2013, p. vii.

2   Ibid., p. 17.

3   One exception that Piketty mentions explicitly is Simon Kuznets, who played a decisive role in establishing the concept of gross domestic product in the first place, and who met with resistance in the United States for a long time. The Second World War and the necessity to plan the war economy made the breakthrough possible. On this and Kuznets, see Philipp Lepenies, *Die Macht der einen Zahl. Eine politische Geschichte des Bruttoinlandsprodukts*, Berlin, 2013.

4   The fact that in a European Central Bank study on wealth, the Forbes list of the world's richest people is used as a source, speaks volumes.

5   Interview with Thomas Piketty, 'Ich brauche das Geld nicht', *die tageszeitung*, June 25, 2014.

6   See topincomes.parisschoolofeconomics.eu.

7   At piketty.pse.ens.fr/en/capital21c2 one finds not only the data

sets, but also explanations concerning the sources of the data and the problems of preparing it.

8 An overview of all the graphics used in Piketty's book can be found here: piketty.pse.ens.fr/files/capital21c/en/Piketty 2014FiguresTablesLinks.pdf.

9 Piketty, p. 43.

10 Ibid., p. 46.

11 Ibid., p. 47.

12 Ibid., p. 48.

13 Ibid., p. 40.

14 Ibid., p. 100f.

15 See Figure 1.2 in Piketty.

16 Karl Marx and Friedrich Engels, *1852–55, Letters*, Lawrence & Wishart, 1983, pp. 50, 55.

17 See Figures 4.1, 4.6, 4.9 and 4.10 in Piketty.

18 Piketty, p. 164.

19 Ibid., p. 344.

20 Compare Figure 10.9 with Figure 10.10 in Piketty.

21 Piketty, p. 498.

22 Ibid., p. 500.

23 Ibid., p. 346.

24 Ibid.

25 Ibid., p. 241.

26 See Figures 5.3 and 5.4 in Piketty.

27 Piketty, p. 508.

28 See Figure 14.1 in Piketty.

29 See Figure 5.5 in Piketty.

30 Stockhammer.

31 See Figure 9.8 in Piketty.

32 See Figure 5.6 in Piketty.

33 Piketty, p. 228.

34 Bastian Brinkmann, 'Das Kapital ist zurück', *Süddeutsche Zeitung*, March 27, 2014.

35 Piketty, p. 484.

36 Ibid., p. 485.

37 See Figure 9.7 in Piketty; Piketty, pp. 315ff, 508ff.

38 Piketty, p. 572.

39 See Figure 5.8 in Piketty; see also Figure 10.10.

40 See Figure 11.12 in Piketty.

41 Piketty, p. 402.

42 Ibid., p. 422.

43 Ibid., p.354ff.

44 Ibid., p. 493.

45 Ibid., p. 471.
46 Ibid., p. 474ff.
47 Ibid., p. 479.
48 Ibid., p. 515.
49 Brinkmann.
50 Piketty, p. 572.
51 Ibid., p. 517.
52 Ibid., p. 572.
53 See Figure 14.1 in Piketty.
54 Piketty, p. 527ff.
55 Ibid., p. 521ff.

4. Hype and Critique

1   According to a report by the *Wall Street Journal*, *Capital in the Twenty-First Century* not only ranked at the very top of the bestseller lists, but also occupied the top spot among those books that readers prematurely stop reading (the percentage of readers who stop reading: 97.6 per cent) according to the Amazon data on reader behavior for their e-book reader Kindle. Piketty thus pushed the previous eternal front-runner, Stephen Hawking (*A Brief History of Time*) down to the number 2 spot (93.4 per cent). Jordan Ellenberg, 'The Summer's Most Unread Book Is …', *Wall Street Journal*, July 3, 2014.

2   Stephanie Flanders, 'Capital in the Twenty-first Century by Thomas Piketty – Review', *Guardian*, July 17, 2014.

3   Quotes from the Preface to Ulrich Horstmann, *Alles was über 'Das Kapital im 21. Jahrhundert' von Thomas Piketty wissen müssen*, FinanzBuch Verlag, 2014. Similar remarks were made by Gerald Braunberger on the *FAZ-Blog*.

4   Paul Krugman, 'Why We're in a New Gilded Age', *New York Review of Books*, May 8, 2014.

5   All quotes are from the Introduction to Horstmann, 2014.

6   Hans-Werner Sinn, 'Thomas Pikettys Weltformel', *FAZ*, May 13, 2014.

7   Similar arguments are made by Stefan Homburg, 'Critical Remarks on Piketty's "Capital in the Twenty-First Century"', *Applied Economics* 47, pp. 1401–06.

8   Karl Brenke, 'Einkommensumverteilung schwächt privaten Verbrauch', Wochenbericht des DIW Berlin Nr. 8, 2011.

9   Albert F. Reiterer, *Der Piketty-Hype – 'The Great U-Turn'. Piketty's Kapital und die neoliberale Vermögenskonzentration*, pad-verlag, 2014.

10 Fabian Lindner, 'Verschärft der Kapitalismus die Ungleichheit oder nicht? -Thomas Piketty vs. Peter Bofinger', *Die Zeit* blog, June 5, 2014.

11 Clive Crook, 'The Most Important Book Ever Is All Wrong', *BloombergView*, April 20, 2014.

12 Daron Acemoğlu and James A. Robinson, 'The Rise and Decline of General Laws of Capitalism', *Journal of Economic Perspectives*, 29:1, 2015, 3–28.

13 Piketty, p. 27.

14 *Wirtschaftswoche*, June 1, 2014.

15 *Manager Magazin* online, April 30, 2014.

16 *Süddeutsche Zeitung*, May 17, 2014

17 Ibid.

18 Piketty, p. 19.

19 Chris Giles and Ferdinando Giugliano, 'Thomas Piketty's Exhaustive Inequality Data Turn Out To Be Flawed', *Financial Times*, May 23, 2014.

20 Piketty response to FT data concerns, *Financial Times*, May 23, 2014.

21 Scott Winship, 'The Financial Times is Blowing Piketty's Data Issues Out of Proportion, Part One', *Forbes*, May 27, 2014.

22 Larry Elliot, 'FT Journalist Accused of Serious Errors in Thomas Piketty Takedown', *Guardian*, May 29, 2014.

23 Ulrike Herrmann, 'Vorsprung durch Tautologie', *Berliner Republik*, March 2014.

24 His book, *The Hidden Wealth of Nations: The Scourge of Tax Havens*, was published in English in 2015.

25 Institute der deutschen Wirtschaft Köln, 'Entwicklung von Ungleichkeit und Armut in Deutschland', April 2010.

26 Philip Vermeulen, *How Fat Is the Top Tail of Wealth Distribution?* European Central Bank Working Paper Series No. 1692, July 2014.

27 Jakob Kapeller, *The Return of the Rentier*, ICAE Working Paper Series No. 26, July 2014.

28 Benjamin Kunkel, 'Paupers and Richlings', *London Review of Books*, 36:13, July 3, 2014, and James K. Galbraith, 'Kapital for the Twenty-First Century?', *Dissent*, Spring 2014.

29 Piketty, p. 230ff.

30 David Harvey, 'Afterthoughts on Piketty's Capital', davidharvey.org, May 17, 2014.

31 Rainer Rilling, 'Die Ungleichheitsmaschine', *Telepolis*, September 6, 2014.

32 Doug Henwood, 'The Top of the World', *Bookforum*, April/May 2014.
33 David Graeber, 'Savage Capitalism Is Back – and It Will Not Tame Itself', *Guardian*, May 30, 2014.
34 Joachim Bischoff and Bernhard Müller, *Piketty's 'Kapital im 21. Jahrhundert'. Der modern Kapitalismus = eine oligarchische Gesellschaft?*, Supplement der Zeitschrift Sozialismus, September 2014, p. 9.
35 Hagen Krämer, 'Piketty, das Kapital und die Arbeit', *Die Zeit* blog, July 14, 2014.
36 Bischoff and Müller.
37 Chandran Nair, 'Inequality and the Nature of Capital: A Reminder to Economists', YaleGlobal Online, June 17, 2014.
38 Piketty, p. 460ff.
39 topincomesg-mond.parisschoolofeconomics.eu.

5. *Capital in the Twenty-First Century* – What to Make of It?

1   Mark Whitehouse, 'It Doesn't Matter if Piketty Is Wrong', *BloombergView*, May 28, 2014.
2   Reiterer.
3   Organisation for Economic Co-operation and Development, *Shifting Gear: Policy Challenges for the Next 50 Years*, OECD Economics Department Policy Notes, No. 24, July 2014.
4   On this debate, see Nicola Liebert, *Steuergerechtigkeit in der Globalisierung*, Verlag Westfälisches Dampfboot, 2011.
5   Gerald Braunberger, 'Ökonomen im Gespräch (6): Thomas Piketty über seine Bewunderung des Kapitalismus', Fazit – das Wirtschaftsblog, May 25, 2014.
6   See Sabine Nuss, *Copyright & Copyriot*, Verlag Westfälisches Dampfboot, 2006, p. 134ff and Uwe Wesel, 'Die Entwicklung des Eigentums in früheren Gesellschaften', Zeitschrift für vergleichende Rechtswissenschaft, 81. Jg, H.1, 1982, p. 24ff.
7   Karl Marx and Friedrich Engels, *Economic Works, 1857–61*, Lawrence & Wishart, 1986, p. 399.
8   Karl Marx, *Capital, Volume 2*, Penguin, 1978, p. 120.
9   Karl Marx, *Capital, Volume 1*, Penguin, 1976, p. 554, fn. 14.
10 John Locke, *Second Treatise on Government*, Hackett Publishing Company, 1980, p. 19.
11 Piketty, p. 422.
12 Gert G. Wagner, 'Leistung und gerechter Lohn: "Am Arbeitsmarkt gibt es keine Gerechtigkeit"', *Berliner Zeitung*, April 18, 2014.

13 Gert Wagner interview with Stephan Kaufmann and Eva Roth, 'Leistung und gerechter Lohn "Am Arbeitsmarkt gibt es keine Gerechtigkeit"', *Berliner Zeitung*, April 18, 2014.

14 Isaac Chotiner, 'Thomas Piketty: I Don't Care for Marx', *New Republic*, May 6, 2014.

15 Piketty, p. 422.

16 Ibid., p. 417.

17 Göran Therborn, *The Killing Fields of Inequality*, Cambridge, 2013, pp. 13, 26.

18 Giorgos Stephanopoulos, 'Faule Griechen, fitte Deutsche', *ZAG antirassistische Zeitschrift*, Nr. 60, 2012.

19 Stephan Kaufmann, Ökonomische Krise als Charakterfrage, Prokla 140, 2005.

20 See Jeremy Brecher, *Strike!: Revised and Expanded*, PM Press, 2014; Francis Fox Piven and Richard A. Cloward, *Poor People's Movements: Why They Succeed, How They Fail*, Vintage, 1978; Robert S. McElvaine, *The Great Depression: America, 1929–1941*, Crown, 1984.

Index

Index

Printed in the United States
by Baker & Taylor Publisher Services